MARY SHELLEY

Starmont Reader's Guide 36

• • • • • • • • • • • • • • •

Allene Stuart Phy

Series Editor, Roger C. Schlobin

STARMONT HOUSE, INC.
1988

Library of Congress Cataloging in Publication Data:

Phy, Allene Stuart.
  Mary Shelley.

  (Starmont reader's guide ; 36)
  Bibliography: p.
  Includes index.
  1. Shelley, Mary Wollstonecraft, 1797-1851—Criticism and
interpretation. I. Title. II. Series.
  PR5398.P4 1988   823'.7   86-6502
  ISBN 0-930261-61-5 (cloth)
  ISBN 0-930261-60-7 (paper)

ALLENE STUART PHY has taught in Africa and has worked with the Peace Corps on programs in language and literature for Zaire, Kenya, and Liberia. Her post-doctoral studies have taken her to universities in four foreign countries, and she has conducted travel seminars in Italy and the Soviet Union. For several years she taught the history of religions, comparative literature, and children's literature at George Peabody College, Vanderbilt University. She was primarily involved in the training of teachers for all levels of instruction. The author of many articles and translations, Phy has also been a staff book reviewer for *School Library Journal*, *Fantasy Review*, the Nashville *Tennessean*, and Montgomery *Advertiser*, and other popular and academic publications. Her books include *The Bible and Popular Culture in America*, published by Fortress Press. Currently Professor of English at Alabama State University, she is now collaborating with her husband, Prof. Frederick B. Olsen, on a book about science fiction and world religions.

FIRST EDITION

CONTENTS

To the Memory of
A. Edwin Anderson,
Beloved Teacher and Mentor

I
CANON AND CHRONOLOGY

1797   Mary is born in London on August 30 at 11:20 P.M. to the philosopher and author William Godwin and his bride of five months, Mary Wollstonecraft, also a well-known novelist and thinker. The mother has a difficult delivery and dies of a resulting infection on September 10.

1801   After several abortive attempts to find a suitable stepmother for his small daughter and for Fanny, Mary Wollstonecraft's child by Gilbert Imlay, Godwin marries his neighbor, Mrs. Mary Jane Clairmont. Mrs. Clairmont brings into the household a son, Charles, and a daughter, Jane, later to be known as Claire.

1803   A son, William, is born to Godwin and his second wife.

1805   The Godwins struggle for a living. At Mrs. Godwin's suggestion, they start a publishing firm specializing in children's books, known as the Juvenile Library. This venture, like others, suffers as a result of Godwin's lack of business expertise. Mary, a lonely child, "scribbles" during her recreational hours. She meets literary and intellectual personalities of the day when they frequent the Godwin home.

1812   As a probable result of the antagonism between Mary and Mrs. Godwin, but ostensibly for her health, Godwin arranges for Mary to live in Dundee, Scotland, with a local family, the Baxters. She is to remain with them for almost two years, a relatively happy period. Mary continues to write. On November 11, during a visit home to London, Mary meets Percy Bysshe Shelley and his wife Harriet, who are visiting the Godwins.

1814   On March 10, Mary returns to live in the Godwin household. On May 5 she again meets Shelley there. Convincing her that his marriage to Harriet is over, Shelley persuades Mary to elope with him to the Continent. Stepsister Jane changes her name to Claire and joins their party. They travel through France, Switzerland, Germany, and Holland and later write of their adventures in *History of a Six Weeks Tour*, which they will publish anonymously three years later. On September 14, they are forced by financial circumstances to return to England.

1815 A female child is born prematurely to Mary and Shelley. A few days later, on March 6, the child dies.

1816 A second child, a son named William and affectionately called "Wilmouse," is born to Mary and Shelley. With Claire Clairmont, they settle in Geneva, Switzerland, near the residence of Lord Byron and his personal physician, Dr. John Polidori. Claire conceives a child by Byron. Matthew (Monk) Lewis, the writer of popular Gothic horror stories, pays a visit, inspiring the entire company to attempt writing Gothic fiction. Mary begins work on *Frankenstein*. In August she returns to England with Shelley and Claire. Mary's half-sister, Fanny, commits suicide by taking poison or October 11. In December Harriet Westbrook Shelley, still the legal wife of Percy Bysshe, drowns herself in the Serpentine. Shelley marries Mary in church on December 30, twenty days after Harriet's body is recovered from the river. He seeks custody of his two children by Harriet.

1817 The Shelleys live in Marlow for a time. Another daughter, Clara Everina, is born on September 2. Claire Clairmont's daughter by Lord Byron, Allegra, is born.

1818 *Frankenstein* is published anonymously on March 11. The Shelley party decides to return to the Continent, where the child Clara dies in Venice on September 24.

1819 The Shelleys settle for a time in Rome, a setting they will use in their writings. On June 7, little William dies. In November, Mary completes a novella, *Matilda*, which Godwin disapproves of—he makes no effort to publish the story in England. On November 12, while living in Florence, Mary gives birth to her only child who is to survive, Percy Florence.

1820 Mary writes two blank-verse dramas, adapted from Ovid, *Persephine* and *Midas*.

1821 Mary and Shelley acquire an important circle of associates at Pisa. They meet Countessa Emilia Viviani who inspires Shelley to Platonic love and Mary to satirical literary composition.

1822 Allegra dies in Venice on April 19. In June, Mary suffers a painful miscarriage. One tragedy follows another. Shelley drowns on July 8, during a sailing expedition with Edward Williams and Charles Vivian. Mary expresses her grief and guilt in the poem "The Choice." Shelley's body is cremated, and his ashes are taken to the Protestant Cemetery in Rome.

1823   On February 25, Mary publishes her novel based on Italian history, *Valperga*. In August she returns to England to make her home, hoping for the assistance of Shelley's father, Sir Timothy. She discovers that the stage version of *Frankenstein* is a success, and she is well known at home.

1824   Mary, who has dedicated herself to the preservation of her husband's memory, publishes her edition of Shelley's posthumous poems. After only three hundred copies have been sold, Sir Timothy threatens to withdraw his meager support of Percy Florence unless the rest of the edition is suppressed. Mary is forced to comply with his demands.

1824   Mary leads a quiet life as a writer. At her father's home, she meets celebrated authors, including the Americans, James Fenimore Cooper and Washington Irving. She experiences a mild infatuation with Irving.

1825   Mary manages, after many negotiations and with Lord Byron's assistance, to obtain a 100-pound annuity from the Shelley family for the support of her son.

1826   Mary's apocalyptic novel and second most influential work, *The Last Man*, is published. Charles Bysshe Shelley, the son of Shelley and Harriet and heir to the family title and estate, dies and Percy Florence, the surviving son, becomes the official heir.

1828   Mary is invited to give a series of lectures in Paris. She falls ill with a mild case of smallpox but makes a satisfactory recovery. She develops warm friendships in French literary and social circles, meets Stendhal, General Lafayette, and other giants of the period. Prosper Merimée, the French author of *Carmen*, becomes her friend and suitor.

1829   Mary begins a ten-year period of publishing short narratives, most of them in the popular, rather-sentimental British annual, *Keepsake*.

1830   *Perkin Warbeck*, Mary's novel on British Tudor history, is published. Short stories continue to appear in *Keepsake*.

1832   Mary is at work on an Italian series of *Lives* for the

Rev. Dionysius Lardner's *Cabinet Cyclopedia*.   Mary'
half-brother, William Godwin, dies in July.

1833   In April Mary goes to live at Harrow where Perc;
Florence is a day-student.

1835   *Lodore*, a novel generally regarded as a fictionaliza
tion of personalities in the Shelley-Byron set, i
published. Mary contributes biographical sketches o
notable Italians to Larder's *Cabinet Cyclopedia*.

1836   William Godwin dies on April 7. Mary is literar;
executor and plans a biography to preserve his fame
though she is never able to complete it. She valiant
ly proceeds to make provisions for the stepmother sh
has never liked.

1837   *Falkner*, a sentimental novel about the devotion of
foundling girl to a Byronic hero, is published. Mar;
contributes additional lives of Spanish and Portugues
worthies to Lardner's *Cyclopedia*.

1838   Several French lives by Mary are published in th
Lardner series. She contemplates full-length biogra
phies of the Empress Josephine, Madame de Stael, an
the Prophet Mohamet. She works on a biography of he
late husband, and edits his poems.

1839   Volume II of Lardner's series of French *Lives* i
published, with contributions by Mary. Her edition o
Shelley's *Poetical Works* is published in four volumes
A second, more complete, edition follows. Mary edit
and publishes prose works by Shelley, under the titl
*Essays, Letters from Abroad, Translations and Frag
ments*.

1840-41   Mary maintains personal and literary friendships wit
emerging Victorian literary figures. She assists Tho
mas Moore in editing the words of Byron. Her associ
ates now include Bulwer-Lytton, Disraeli, Samuel Ri
hards, and Abraham Hayward. She travels again in Eu
rope.

1843   Mary revisits Italy, including Florence, Rome and Sor
rento.

1844   At the death of Sir Timothy, Percy Florence inherit
his title and a substantial income. The years t
follow are comfortable for Mary. Percy Florence mee
Jane St. John, a widow devoted to Shelley's memor;
Mary publishes her travel book, *Rambles in Germany an
Italy*, in two volumes.

1845	Mary has difficulties with a literary forger and a would-be blackmailer. She deals wisely with "Major" Byron, a disreputable character who preys upon vulnerable celebrities.
1848	On June 22, Percy Florence marries Jane St. John. They establish a Shelley shrine in their home.
1851	Mary dies on February 1, in her home in London, Chester Square, after a period of declining health and eight days in a coma. As she has requested, she is buried in St. Peter's Churchyard, Bournemouth, between the graves of her father and mother.

II
THE PROBLEM OF MARY SHELLEY

In 1932, James Whale of Universal Studios identified the author of *Frankenstein* merely as "Mrs. Percy Bysshe Shelley." Whale appears to have regarded his film, with its own Karloffian monster, as a vastly more effective vehicle for conveying the strange narrative in which the Gothic sensibility is wedded with the scientific than was a quaint early-nineteenth century romance. In his sequel, *The Bride of Frankenstein*, Whale not only acknowledged "Mary Wollstonecraft Shelley" but even introduced her as a character played by Elsa Lancaster. Perhaps he was beginning to realize that without her inspiration he might never have established himself as Hollywood's greatest director of horror films.

Outside the movie, Mary Wollstonecraft Godwin Shelley has not been ignored. Numerous books and articles have been written about her, from all established critical perspectives and from several unorthodox ones. The critical bibliography is, in fact, enormous.

Yet what impresses the reader of this large body of interpretation is the elusiveness of the subject, despite her often-highly confessional writings and the abundant detailing of her life by others. Earlier studies tended to view Mary chiefly as the wife of a major English poet, much as Whale initially regarded her. Other critics have seen her as little more than a minor member of one of the intriguing circles of the British Romantic Movement in literature. Occasionally a scholar has found Mary interesting chiefly for her association with Lord Byron, a more titillating figure of that circle than Shelley himself. Byron's dashing image is, of course, as familiar in popular lore as in English poetry. The "Byronic" heroes of Mary's own fiction have sometimes received undue attention to the neglect of more important and original features of her work.

Mary's unconventional early life in and out of wedlock with Percy Bysshe Shelley has suggested to some biographers that she was a female counterpart of that hero of Romantic mythology, the rebel who defies the expectations of society to follow the dictates of his heart.

Literary historians have been ready to acknowledge Mary Shelley's significance as a minor novelist of her period, what we would call today "a popular writer," whose work provides a mirror of her time, to be scrutinized by students of cultural attitudes. Her travel writings and short stories, as well as her novels, indeed, do respond to the aesthetically aspiring, yet highly-sentimental tastes of the common reader of her time.

A more contemporary interpretation of Mary stresses the courageous solitary woman, widowed early in life, who was seeking to earn a living, rear a child, and establish her independence. Feminists do not forget that she was the daughter of that germinal philosopher of women's rights, Mary Wollstonecraft Godwin, and of William Godwin, political and social liberationist. They point out (*Ms.* is the customary forum) that Mary's writing constantly reflects the ideas of her parents, while the lifestyle she chose during each period of her existence reveals an attempt to practice the feminist standards her mother advocated.

Now, in the closing decades of the twentieth century, it is evident that Mary Shelley is important chiefly because she composed at the age of nineteen one of the most extraordinary books ever written, *Frankenstein: or the Modern Prometheus*. Few family names are better known throughout the Western world than that of the ill-fated scientist of her book. Yet millions fail to associate the cinematic Frankenstein or his Monster, though their fame continues to spread, with the rather quiet woman who is still often identified as the widow of an English poet.

Unlike movie audiences throughout the world, readers of the present volume are certain to know that Mary Shelley created the Monster who first escaped from the pages of her novel to posture and terrify on stage and has continued to run amok on movie screens since the 1930's. These readers are likely also to have read Brian Aldiss and other historians of science fiction who have accorded Mary the title "Founder" of this genre, which seeks to make what is otherwise fantastic plausible by grounding it in science, pseudo-science, or conceivable future science. Of special interest now may be additional information about the genesis of *Frankenstein*, its subsequent stage and film history, and its varied critical interpretations. The other activities of the woman who created a modern myth, particularly the further excursions into literary fantasy and "science fiction," seem more significant than ever.

It has been said again and again, sometimes by the likes of Stephen King, that Mary Shelley's original narratives disappoint. Her writings seem too long on talk and too slow on action. The major Frankenstein movies, with their archetypal images and motifs, have been a part of popular culture for six decades, and the two latest generations of young people have met the Monster and his scientist maker on *The Creature Feature* or *The Late, Late Show*. Viewers today have become acquainted as well with the many sons, brides, returns, and resurrections of both man and Monster. The Hammer films arrived from Britain in the 1950's, two decades after Universal Studios had produced their classic horror pictures. Yet despite the popularity of the Hammer technicolor extravaganzas, with their splattering blood and putrifying flesh, they were unable to erase from public consciousness the image of Boris Karloff as the Monster. Film enthusiasts eagerly approaching Mary's novel have found very different images there and a heavy weight of serious philosophical reflection. Usually they

12

have been disappointed, at least at first. All too few ever returned for a maturer reading. For the book is unlike any film ever made, no matter how loudly the publicists may have asserted that a particular Frankenstein adaptation has been "the true story" or how often an actress playing Mary herself may have appeared in a prologue introducing a new version and pleading its authenticity.

One mark of Mary Shelley's power is certainly the ability of her writing to beget scenarios quite unlike her book. Successful adaptations across media do not slavishly follow an original; they must, rather, exploit the possibilities provided by the new medium. They will also express the artistic vision of the translator into the new medium. There are many ways of exploring a theme, and different themes may be generated by the same dazzling images or initial conceptions. Tracing the Monster through his several transmogrifications becomes one of the more spirited features of *Frankenstein* study.

This book is designed primarily for the general reader, especially the one who enjoys science fiction and fantasy and believes these genres carry significance. The documentation provided should be useful to high school and college teachers, as well as to any student who might be examining *Frankenstein*, the English Romantic Movement, or the currents of British and American popular culture. For convenience and to avoid confusion when referring to several people with similar names, the author of *Frankenstein* will be identified as "Mary" or "Mary Shelley" in most instances, while her husband will be "Percy Bysshe" or simply "Shelley." "Wollstonecraft" and "Godwin" will refer to the parents of Mary Shelley.

Because she is a personality in English literary history, the entire life and body of work of Mary Shelley will be surveyed. Yet special emphasis will be placed on those writings which may be designated without absurdity as "fantasy" or "science fiction." Not only will these writings be of the most interest to the likely reader of this volume; they are also the most valuable of the entire corpus. Since *Frankenstein* is recognized to be of crucial significance, it will receive more attention than any other work, with biographical, psychoanalytic, feminist, sociological, theological, and other serious interpretations briefly reviewed. And because *Frankenstein* has also generated a contemporary mythology, it will be examined also as an artifact of popular culture.

Of the making of books about the Shelleys and *Frankenstein*, there seems to be no end in sight. The work of other scholars need not be imitated or duplicated, and the annotated bibliography of secondary sources will direct readers to sources where their particular interests will be satisfied. This volume seeks to provide, in readily accessible form, a concise overview of Mary's literary work, along with an assessment of her importance to English literature and popular culture. Though it is generally conceded that Mary occupies a significant place in Western popular thought, her more recent biographers and literary interpreters have suggested that her precise status is yet to be determined. Even the majority view, which holds that her books are seriously flawed (despite an occasional brilliant idea or unforgetable image) is being challenged by those who feel she is a more skilled prose stylist and overall woman-of-letters than generally recognized. Perhaps this new look at her life and total career will help each reader decide how much attention this interesting, capable, and sometimes disturbing woman deserves.

III
THE LIFE AND ACHIEVEMENTS

PARENTS

Children and spouses of celebrated, controversial people develop many strategies for coping with the family relationships, which may be experienced as both burdens and strokes of fortune. Mary's interpreters do not agree when evaluating the effect on her life and career of having two famous parents and an immensely talented husband. If *Frankenstein* is to be regarded as her only work of lasting merit, it is hard to deny that the living presence and encouragement of Percy Shelley were essential to her highest artistic achievement. But it is also possible to wonder if Mary's potential brilliance, glimpsed in her teenage composition of that extraordinary work of fiction, were not stifled by her lifelong self-effacement before the relatives she regarded as far more gifted than herself.

The melodrama of Mary's life begins with her parents. She was the admiring daughter of the poor but prominent philosopher and novelist William Godwin, and neither his later denunciations of her elopement with Shelley nor his greedy supplications to her husband could damper what she acknowledged as the "extravagant and romantic" affection she always bore for him.

Though her mother died a few days after her birth, Mary proudly read all Mary Wollstonecraft's writings, almost as soon as she acquired the skill, and Mary cherished her mother's portrait, which even the second Mrs. Godwin could not banish from its central place in the family parlor. When Mary added "Wollstonecraft" to her own name, in honor of her mother, she made matters difficult for certain future students of literature and hosts on Masterpiece Theatre, who have tended since to confuse the two women. It is significant to recall that when Mary met Shelley and fell in love for the first time, she conducted her courtship at her mother's tomb. Even at the end, following her own request, she was laid to her final rest beside the mother she scarcely knew in the flesh.

Years before Mary's birth, the youthful experiences of Wollstonecraft were to form the basis of a set of books that influenced not only her daughter but all English-speaking society. Born of a meek, browbeaten mother and a brutish father who had squandered the family inheritance by his restlessness and instability, Wollstonecraft took responsibility for her siblings, assisting them as best she could. As soon as she felt her duties were complete, she escaped the miserable household and ventured forth alone.

Though she was without formal education, Wollstonecraft, at one time or another, supported herself by plying all the trades considered suitable for a middle-class woman without means. She labored as companion, seamstress, teacher, and governess. Her experiences as a teacher provided the matter for *Thoughts on the Education of a Daughter*, a writing that first brought her serious public attention and even financial remuneration.

The French Revolution, which started in 1790, moved the idealistic Wollstonecraft deeply with its ringing call for "liberty, equality, and fraternity." She translated revolutionary writings and wrote an answer to Edmond Burke's *Reflections on the French Revolution.* She published her reply to Burke anonymously under the title *A Vindication of the Rights of Men.* When a second edition of her revolutionary credo was published the following year, she used her own name and quickly found herself much discussed in intellectual circles. That same year she met William Godwin for the first time, though initially they made little impression on one another. He complained that she talked too much: undoubtedly, he wanted to do the talking himself. For her part, she was too enamored of the artist Henry Fuseli to notice another man. Obsessed with Fuseli, a bisexual who had given her little encouragement and who had recently married, Wollstonecraft proposed to his wife a *menage à trois*, suggesting for herself the role of Platonic lover. Understandably, Mrs. Fuseli refused with indignation to entertain such a proposition.

Humiliated and lovelorn, Wollstonecraft journeyed to Paris, a city in which she hoped to experience both social liberation and intellectual exhilaration. Still stung by the rejection of the Fuselis, she started a liaison with an American adventurer, Gilbert Imlay, and was soon expecting his child. Though she lavished all the love of her passionate and hitherto repressed spirit on Imlay, he appears to have regarded her as little more than a convenience. He was soon plotting his escape, and by the time their daughter Fanny was born, he was openly demanding release from the increasingly domestic shackles.

Pathetically attempting to retain some hold on Imlay, Wollstonecraft made foreign business excursions on his behalf and offered to share him with his new mistress. Rejected again, she unsuccessfully tried suicide twice.

Literary productivity was maintained despite adversity. No matter how miserable Wollstonecraft's life became, she usually managed to wrench from her agony a few insights, which were then incorporated into a new treatise. About this time she started work on *The Wrongs of Woman*, which was to be her most famous writing. By now, she felt that she had plenty of first-hand experience to add to her theoretical precepts and observations of the deprivations of others. While recovering from the Imlay adventure, she also met Godwin again.

This time both parties were responsive. They discovered that they shared a passion for social justice and basic beliefs about the way it should be achieved, though there remained the less basic philosophical differences any two strongly individualistic people could expect. While Godwin had been an ardent atheist for several years, Wollstonecraft had practiced Anglicanism in her earlier life and had based some of the arguments of her most carefully reasoned treatises on Christian principles. By now, however, she was no longer a communicant. It was, anyhow, more important that she shared with Godwin the excitement of exploring ideas by expressing them in writing.

In print Godwin had already repudiated the institution of matrimony. Since Wollstonecraft was also by now on record with her own reservations, they did not decide to wed until she became pregnant. Even then, they seemed embarrassed to be compromising their principles, and they maintained separate living quarters almost until the time of the baby's birth. The prospect of a child pleased them immensely; certain it would be a boy, they agreed on the name William. Wollstonecraft had delivered her first born, under less auspicious circumstances, with no difficulty, and she anticipated none this time.

Mary was born in her father's living quarters, according to schedule, on August 30, 1797. Eleven days later, Wollstonecraft died miserably of childbed infection.

Godwin saw no better way to honor his wife's memory and assuage his grief than to prepare her writings for posthumous publication, a pattern of behavior his daughter would later follow in her own widowhood. Though Godwin's intentions were honorable, Wollstonecraft's newly released papers demonstrated more fully her unorthodox life to those who were all too ready to dismiss her ideas as the justification of an irresponsible woman for her Bohemian conduct. Even today, there are those willing to drag her from the tomb to their psychiatric couches to label her "an extreme neurotic of the compulsive type." (1)

Yet Wollstonecraft's reputation has survived. Not only was she courageous, industrious, and constantly creative, but she was one of England's most important popularizers of ideas. Some of her doctrines have been rephrased by the American Civil Rights Movement of our own period, logically applied to the plight of the American Black. Her critique of women's problems has proven to be surprisingly contemporary, and feminists continue to value her as a germinal thinker.

Since her teachings were to be so influential on her daughter's writing, it is well to summarize the most important doctrines. Wollstonecraft believed that all social exploitation resulted from the unfair distribution of property and the greed of privileged classes in demanding more than could be rightfully attained from their own labor. She firmly held that education and aspirations rather than natural endowments or the circumstances of birth make people what they are. When inferior education, for example, is given to females, there are dire results: rich women are kept in luxury as playthings, while poorer women are regarded as trusted servants. In both groups women are stifled, and the potential for meaningful relationships between men and women is never realized. Wollstonecraft regarded the sexual

17

double standard as outrageous, in allowing promiscuity to males but demanding absolute chastity of females, even though they might have been forced by circumstances into unions with men they could not love and were never permitted to divorce.

Yet Mary's mother lived in hope, believing that society could be improved and the betterment of relationships was possible. She saw very clearly that, in any situation where exploitation exists, the oppressor suffers as well as the oppressed. If men could accept "rational fellowship" from women rather than "slavish obedience," she contended, they would acquire "more observant daughters, more affectionate sisters, more faithful wives, more reasonable mothers." (2)

Mary Shelley was to echo these ideas throughout her life, even in unexpected contexts. Ironically, despite her brave cry of independence, Wollstonecraft had allowed herself to be demeaned by Imlay. And, biology indeed proved to be her destiny, when she suffered a characteristically female death in childbirth.

Bereft of her mother, Mary grew up worshipping Godwin, beyond question the primary influence of her early life. Although literary and social historians of the period almost consistently paint an unattractive portrait of him, he could not have been totally lacking in paternal virtue and good will. Both daughters of Mary Wollstonecraft loved him dearly, and Fanny's later suicide seems to have been motivated in part by her discovery that she was not his biological daughter.

Godwin's background had been more fortunate than that of his wife. The son of a dissenting Calvinist minister, he had been reared in a protective, loving family. In youth, impressed by his father's vocation, he had trained for the ministry. Yet after serving briefly in a pulpit, he had experienced a radical transformation of heart and mind and had subsequently established himself in London as a philosophical rebel. Lavish in his schemes, even for a century that delighted in grandiose visions of the perfectibility of human beings, he prophesied a social revolution, to be attained by calm discussion and passive resistance to injustice, rather than by violence. Very soon, he renounced all churches and proclaimed himself a total atheist. His protest against that other important social institution, matrimony, was soon to be weakened by his marriages, to Wollstonecraft and, upon her death, to Mrs. Clairmont.

Godwin was a reader of novels and especially enjoyed those of the American master of Gothic intrigue, Charles Brockton Brown. Mary was later to imitate her father's own habit of embodying ideas in vividly imaginative fiction. Though not a creative talent of the highest order, Godwin was cleverly innovative. In 1794 he published *Things as They Are, Or The Adventures of Caleb Williams*, an unusual narrative, filled with provocative ideas. *Caleb* has been identified by some literary historians as the first full-length fictional study of the criminal mind. If this be accurate, Godwin is a precursor of two genuine literary geniuses, Poe and Dostoevsky. He was beyond question the artistic as well as biological father of Mary Shelley. In *Caleb*, Godwin presented in narrative form the doctrines he had outlined in his tract on political justice. He criticized penal conditions, denounced oppression by the privileged classes, and demonstrated the powerful influence of environment on character.

St. Leon, another much-discussed novel, reflected Godwin's keen interest in the occult. Mary thus came by her own occult literary enthusiasm honorably. Sentimental and cluttered though the narrative was, *St. Leon* did dramatize its author's belief that brotherhood and the simple life can bring happiness and peace, a view unimagined by those who seek to control their fortunes through the "philosopher's stone or the occultists' "elixir of life."

Godwin's philosophy of anarchism, fully developed in other writings, influenced many philosophers, several more eloquent and persuasive than he, and profoundly touched a whole generation of English Romantic poets. Though Godwin was not above cultivating the rich and titled for his personal gain, his writings, in that age of revolution, witnessed his conviction that all humans were of equal value in the ultimate scheme of things. He believed that mankind was perfectible, even if incapable of absolute perfection. He agreed heartily with Wollstonecraft that character is primarily the product of education. The greatest forces for the perpetuation of injustice, he asserted, were man-made institutions, which he saw everywhere to be restricting and corrupting. In the ideal society, such institutions as centralized government, social hierarchies, and, of course, marriage would be abolished as unnecessary. The church would probably die a natural death. A new kingless state would emerge where custom would impose no restrictions on the individual's fullest development. People would need to work a mere hour or two each day, with the rest of their time free for the cultivation of intellect and spirit. Punishment for wrongdoing would be abolished, as it would become unnecessary in this ideal society of well behaved and happy people. Property, that other prime source of corruption, would be held by all in common.

Though his Utopia sounds much like the ideal state envisioned by later Communism, Godwin rejected violent revolution, and he would never have condoned the restraints on individualism that totalitarian socialist states in our own century have invariably imposed.

Revering her father as she did, it is certain that Mary entertained from early childhood the ideas that floated in the air of the Godwin home. An examination of her later writings reveals that no major precept of Godwinism escaped her attention. Each was respectfully examined, sometimes adopted, sometimes modified, and sometimes even thoughtfully replaced by what she was convinced was a clearer, more workable doctrine. The personality of Godwin also haunts her books. Even if characters were not always recognizable portraits of her father, they frequently gave Godwinian speeches or, in off moments, spoke in his cadences.

With Wollstonecraft and Godwin as parents, Mary started life with sound heredity and a heritage in which she was always to take immense pride.

Godwin's grief in widowhood was heightened by his feeling of inadequacy as sole parent of the two small daughters of his deceased wife. Despite his bluster about marriage, he sought very quickly to find a suitable step-mother for his daughters, someone who would also be a companion for himself. His rejection by the first two ladies he approached did not long deter him.

Mrs. Mary Jane Clairmont, who called herself a widow, though there remains some mystery about her past, lived next door to Godwin with her own two children, Charles and Jane. One evening, according to the traditional account, she appealed to Godwin's vanity, leaning from her balcony to address him. "Is this the immortal Mr. Godwin?" she is supposed to have asked. After a brief courtship, Mrs. Clairmont became the second Mrs. Godwin.

Assessments of Mary Jane Clairmont Godwin's character and personality, provided by visitors to the home, were not usually complimentary. Yet she seems to have possessed some attractiveness and intelligence, and Godwin appears to have lived with her in reasonable harmony. The year after their marriage, she bore Godwin's only son, William, the sole child in that mixed household attended by his two natural parents. Young William became, from all accounts, insufferable.

It is unlikely that any woman would have pleased Mary as Godwin's wife. Her imagination was alive with wicked stepmother tales, and the idealized mental image of her own mother made a suitable replacement impossible. Even had the new Mrs. Godwin been a saint, Mary's classic Electra complex would have transformed Mary Jane Clairmont into a rival and an enemy.

It is probable that Mrs. Godwin, whatever her intentions may have been, also favored her own children. Mary's pensiveness, lonely imagination, and keen intelligence made her a difficult companion for the Clairmonts, though sister Fanny, less spirited and assertive, seems to have accepted this extended family without complaint.

Jane Clairmont, the new step-sister, who was only slightly younger than Mary, was anxious for compliments and attention. Yet she was much less gifted than her step-sister and lacked the celebrated, canonized mother to whom people were always flatteringly comparing Mary. The two step-sisters developed an ambivalent and perplexing bond which was to be maintained throughout their lives. Jane would act as go-between in Shelley's courtship of Mary, would accompany Mary and Percy on their elopement to the Continent, and would share a *menage* with them for an extended period. She may or may not also have shared Shelley's affections. Many years later, the widowed Mary would assist in publishing some of Jane's writing and would conduct an elaborate, sometimes animated correspondence with her. Yet, nearing the end of her life, Mary would also plead with her daughter-in-law not to leave her alone with Jane, whom she called "the bane of my existence since childhood."

Understandably, Mrs. Godwin was anxious to see that decent provision was made for her family. Despite his international renown, Godwin never seems to have known how to support a family. His new wife urged him to start a publishing firm which would specialize in children's books and be called "The Juvenile Library." Though both husband and wife worked hard, the enterprise was not financially successful, and Godwin was soon reduced to his near-habitual condition of bankruptcy. Whatever the state of his finances, he never lost his stance as an enlightened gentleman philosopher and man of letters looking for an appropriate patron.

In 1812, that momentous year in world affairs, when Napoleon was invading Russia, Godwin sent Mary to live in Dundee with a family of Scottish friends, the William Baxters. While the official explanation was that Mary was moving North for her health, it is quite likely that Godwin wanted a more peaceful home than he had been able to maintain with the constant rivalries between Mary and the Clairmonts. Godwin was proud of his daughter and boasted that people found her quite pretty and bright. Yet he admitted she could be "singularly bold" and "somewhat imperious."

Mary was able to live harmoniously with the Baxters. This stay in Scotland, which lasted almost two years, was later to be remembered as a happy time of youth. She would also make good use in her later fiction of the mystery and romantic gloom she found in the Scottish landscapes.

It was during the Scottish period that a major event took place. Mary came home for a brief visit with the Godwins, who were living on Skinner Street in London. There, for the first time, she met Percy Bysshe Shelley, who was calling on Godwin in the company of his first wife, the radiant and elegant Harriet Westbrook. Shelley had already declared himself a disciple of the philosopher and had initiated a correspondence some time earlier. Godwin too had cultivated the friendship, no doubt flattered by the admiration of a gifted younger man and possibly, even at this early date, alert to the advantages to be gained from association with the son of a nobleman of means. After the meeting, Harriet Westbrook Shelley, with generosity of spirit, described Mary to a friend as "very much like her mother, whose picture hangs up in Godwin's study. She must have been a most lovely woman." (3)

HUSBAND

It was not until 1814 that Mary returned to London to resume her permanent residence with her family. Shelley again called on Godwin. The idealistic and somewhat pretentious young poet seems quickly to have recognized a potential soul mate in this daughter of Wollstonecraft and his mentor. He had already become disenchanted with his marriage to Harriet. Pronouncing her insensitive and crudely *bourgeoise*, he had concluded that she was totally unfit to be consort to one such as himself. Demonstrating his ability to recast the events of his life in conformity to comforting myths, Shelley amended the version of his initial courtship of Harriet that his friends had heard. Now he claimed that he had never thought of her as a spiritual companion but had regarded her as a *protégé* whom he had rescued from parental tyranny. That Harriet's own letters reveal her to have been an unusually intelligent and spirited woman only enchances the tragedy of Shelley's self-delusion and the rejection which ultimately destroyed the first wife. At any rate, within a few months, Shelley was ardently declaring his love for Mary and convincing her that the ties with Harriet were no longer binding.

Events moved quickly. Mary had taken the writings of both her mother and her father seriously; as their ready disciple, she believed in the power of love over the tyranny of social institutions. On July 28, 1814, only four months after her return from Scotland, she eloped to the Continent with the still-married Shelley. Godwin, whose advocacy of free love did not extend to members of his own family, was horrified. No doubt, he also realized that Shelley's actions would anger Sir Timothy Shelley, who would now do his best to disinherit his wayward son. The Shelley connection would thus become less advantageous. Mrs. Godwin was further mortified when she discovered that her own daughter, for reasons that have never been fully clarified, had accompanied the fleeing couple.

Jane Clairmont, who soon chose to call herself by the more poetic name of "Claire," was still the competitive little sister. She may also have harbored an infatuation for Shelley, who was far from oblivious of her charms. Her pictures reveal her to have been dark, plump, and exotically pretty. Certainly Claire wanted to be part of the exciting creative circle of art and poetry which Shelley and Mary soon established around them. Determined to become the mistress, if not the wife, of a great poet, Jane soon succeeded in this goal, to her unhappiness and lasting bitterness.

Now even Godwin and the memory of Wollstonecraft were eclipsed, as Percy Bysshe Shelley became Mary's object of adoration and dominant influence. Her years with him were to be few, for he would die eight years later at age twenty-nine. Yet for the rest of her life, Mary was to define herself as the one he had loved. She would continue to live in his shadow. To understand her and what she achieved, it is necessary to know what nature of man he was.

Shelley was a youthful rebel who died before he had time to indicate what changes maturity would have brought. When Robert Southey, an older, less-inspired Romantic who became poet laureate, met Shelley he felt that he was beholding a vision of himself in youth. Because of Shelley's untimely death, he continues to be remembered for his feverish enthusiasms and sometimes-childish rebellions. Mathew Arnold did not improve this reputation by calling Shelley a beautiful, ineffectual angel beating his wings in the void.

In life, the young poet was a scandal to his family and to the rest of British aristocracy. Even today, despite more tolerant attitudes, his personal life seems only slightly less reprehensible than the majority of his contemporaries viewed it. There is no evidence that he ever felt a pang of remorse for deserting his first wife during her second pregnancy, neglecting his two children by her, and eventually contributing to the troubles that drove her to suicide. Devoted as he was to Mary, his second wife, he was sometimes callous and not always as mindful as he might have been of the health of his second family of children. And he constantly and openly ridiculed and defamed his own father, Sir Timothy.

Not everybody regarded Shelley as completely sane. As a child, he had entertained his brothers and sisters with fantastic and sinister stories. At school, he had experimented so often with alchemy and black magic that he earned the nickname "Mad Shelley." His near-paranoia and irrationality are documented on several oocasions in later life. As an early sign of his precarious grip on reality, it will be remembered that, after being thrown out of Oxford for his radical ideas, he went on a missionary journey to Ireland to convert the good Roman Catholics there to his brand of atheism. Though he loved children and was always ready to offer shelter to homeless ones, his vagabond style of living proved fatal to most who came under his roof. Lord Byron, in removing his natural daughter from the Shelley household, was to express a widely-held opinion that no child could survive in what he called that unwholesome environment of vegetarianism and atheism.

Shelley's views on marriage, though not unlike Godwin's, could hardly have been congenial to Mary's temperament. Advocating what today would be called "open marriage," he is believed to have encouraged the reluctant Mary on at least one occasion to have a flirtation with his friend, Thomas Jefferson Hogg, to whom he had earlier offered his first wife, Harriet. His own amorous adventures, which seem to have been chiefly Platonic (Emilia Viviani was the best known object of his devotion), were celebrated in his poetry. Even if he never became Claire's lover, his obvious liking for Mary's lifetime rival and step-sister could not have made his relationship with his second wife any smoother. Some biographers believe that Shelley also fathered a child by a servant girl and was later subjected to blackmail for that indiscretion. It seems more likely that he was the victim of another of many vicious rumors spread by those who hated or envied him.

Yet there was another side to Shelley's character, almost totally ignored by his enemies but which cannot be neglected if one is to understand Mary's lifelong devotion to his memory. It is a cliché to say a person is "generous to a fault," yet this was the literal truth with Shelley. He was long-suffering, quick to forgive those who wronged him. For years, he endured Godwin's abuse almost without complaint, while he generously responded to his father-in-law's incessant appeals for money, even at times when he could scarcely meet his own needs. Shelley could also be extraordinarily compassionate and hospitable. He was always on the verge of adopting an orphan or tending another sick animal.

Shelley was an exciting, erratic personality, teeming with ideas, plans, and interesting speculations. He spoke of dreams, omens, and incantations; he threatened to raise the dead and evoke spirits and demons, and claimed to chat familiarly with ghosts. He also claimed to have been a lover of Antigone in a previous incarnation. The outer limits of science—the wonders of Dr. Erasmus Darwin, of Galvinism, of electricity—intrigued him. And, he encouraged others to be equally imaginative and creative. A high-born man, Shelley indicated by his admiration for John Keats that he valued character and ability rather than birth and that he could honor talents greater than his own without insidious envy. Since his school days, he had been a sincere advocate of liberty and human betterment. Most acquaintances agreed that Shelley was a graceful human being with many arresting qualities.

His writings demonstrate impressive strengths as well as hurtful weaknesses. His lofty ideals and all-embracing enthusiasms were expressed in verse that was as often loose and vague as it could be lyrically stunning.

Temperamentally atune to Platonic mysticism, Shelley glorified love as a healing, renewing force. In his especially ambitious poem "Queen Mab," he attacked Christianity, which he felt had incited religious intolerance while hypocritically professing this love.

A hatred of tyranny was another of Shelley's motivating passions. Perhaps the dominant idea of his poem "The Revolt of Islam" is that love, understood as both a transcendent and imminent force, will regenerate men, leading them toward a golden age in which there will be a deliverance from all the tyrannies of perverse or imperfect social institutions.

The elopement journey of the Shelleys, with its picaresque rambles through several European countries, was to form the basis for the first part of a work entitled *History of a Six Weeks' Tour*, jointly composed by Mary and Percy and published anonymously in 1817. Accommodations were frequently miserable. In one country inn, the rats drove step-sister Claire (not too regretfully, one suspects) into the bed of the two lovers. At another point Shelley, always an easy touch for suffering children or animals, ended up carrying a feeble little ass he had purchased for the young women to ride. After a time abroad filled with youthful adventure as well as hardship, the elopement party returned to England.

Interested busybodies did not forget that Shelley was still the legal husband of Harriet Westbrook, who was carrying his second child. An added complication was Mary's own pregnancy, now obvious. Understandably, the conservative Shelley family did not look with favor upon one of their members deserting an expectant wife to live with an equally pregnant mistress. The Godwins as well were chagrined by vicious rumors, which were certainly untrue, that the philosopher had sold both his daughters to the wayward poet.

Mary's child, a girl, was born prematurely and died a few days later on March 6, 1815. In August she and Shelley settled at Bishopgate where they were to remain until May of the next year. A second child was born January 24, 1816; they named the boy William in honor of Godwin, who still looked with disfavor on the illicit union, even while he demanded money from Shelley to cover the expenses of his own family.

When spring came, Mary, Shelley, and Claire again headed for the Continent, possibly at the instigation of Claire, who had reasons of her own for wishing to be near Lake Geneva. Their party settled in Geneva, near Lord Byron's residence at Villa Diadoti, famous for its associations with Milton. Lord Byron, shadowed by his much-ridiculed but not untalented personal physician, Dr. John Polidori, became Shelley's constant companion. The party jeeringly referred to the doctor as "pollydolly," perhaps because of his dandyish ways; probably because of these references, Polidori has suffered mightily at the hands of the historical novelists, who delight in making a villain of him. Claire, who had formed an attachment to the increasingly-reluctant Byron while she was still in England, gathered in the evenings with Mary, Shelley, Byron, and the physician to discuss science and pseudo-science and to read German Gothic romances.

FRANKENSTEIN PERIOD

The ideas that were to be expressed in *Frankenstein* germinated from the conversations of these Geneva evenings, Mary was later to recall. In large part it was the ambiance of this time and place that would be so keenly captured in that narrative. The exact details of the book's genesis may have been embellished in Mary's memory or literarily enhanced when she recalled them for the preface to the revised version of the novel several years later. Indeed, independent accounts of those evenings, from the journals of Claire and Dr. Polidori, are not in full accord. Yet the setting and company unquestionably contributed to the weird atmosphere of the work Mary produced. Even Polidori, who was not regarded as especially talented, felt sufficiently inspired to write a vampire tale which is widely regarded as a precursor to Bram Stoker's classic *Dracula*.

In August, Matthew G. "Monk" Lewis arrived in Geneva with a retinue of Jamaican servants. Though he was a diplomat from a highly respectable family, Lewis had become a scandal, a successful author, and an overnight celebrity because of his salacious Gothic romance *The Monk*, a tale of matricide, incest, and sorcery. Far into the night, Lewis discoursed on literature and the occult to the spellbound Byron-Shelley party.

Though Mary was later to remember that "Frankenstein summer" as a golden period of her life, a time of productivity and happiness, it was in reality filled with mounting tensions. Claire was pregnant with Lord Byron's child. Byron, who claimed Claire had inflicted herself upon him, now took a fierce dislike to her and refused even to be alone in her company. Although he was prepared to provide for his child, he made it clear that he would do so only if Claire agreed to renounce almost all her maternal rights.

Always restless in their movements, the Shelley party returned to England, not knowing their lives were soon to be shaken by two suicides. Mary's half-sister, Fanny, died alone in a rented room in Swansea. Like her mother years before, she had decided to end a burdensome existence with a lethal drug dosage; unlike her mother, she had succeeded. Her suicide note, though pathetically self-pitying, did not really explain her action. Long given to moods of depression and feelings of worthlessness she had recently discovered her illegitimacy. She may also have fancied she loved Shelley. Certainly Fanny felt herself an outsider in both the Godwin and Shelley households; even the despised Claire had been granted the affection and protection of Shelley. Upon learning of her death, Godwin responded with shock and embarrassment. He refused to claim her body and told her Wollstonecraft relatives she was away in Ireland. Unattended she was buried in an unmarked pauper's grave, just as if she had no relatives and were not the daughter of a famous woman.

The death of Fanny had been sufficiently guilt-inflicting yet only a short time later the body of Harriet Westbrook Shelley was fished out of the Serpentine. Though she was clearly another suicide, the exact details of Harriet's sordid end have never become fully known. She was again pregnant, though this time almost certainly not by Shelley.

For Mary and Shelley, Harriet's death was simultaneously a shock and a relief. As the surviving parent, Shelley fully expected to be given custody of his two children by Harriet, and Mary prepared to welcome them to the household.

On the advice of his soliciter, Shelley hastened to be honorably married to Mary at St. Mildred's, Bread Street, in London. Yet his new respectability did not impress John Westbrook, the grandfather of the children, a wealthy man who employed skilled legal counsel to assemble a convincing case against Shelley's custody. Not only could Westbrook document with personal letters the irregularities of Shelley's life and his desertion of his first family, but by quoting from Shelley's published writings, he was able to demonstrate religious and political views which the court agreed were dangerous for young children. Shelley was never to succeed in gaining custody of his daughter and son by Harriet.

Mary and Shelley established a residence at Marlow in England and remained there for several months. Now that Mary had the status of a legal wife, Godwin decided to forgive the young couple and even bragged to his family and friends that his daughter, without fortune of her own, had married a wealthy man of high birth. On September 2, 1817, Mary gave birth to her first child in wedlock, a daughter she named Clara Everina.

Frankenstein was published anonymously on March 11, 1818.

and immediately attracted considerable attention in England. The Shelley party, however, had decided to return to Italy, where they felt less social censure and greater creative stimulation. Nevertheless, misfortune followed them. In late September, little Clara died in Venice, possibly a casualty to Shelley's perpetual movement. Though he loved his children dearly, Shelley was never other than a remarkably self-absorbed individual, always convinced that his actions were right and correct. He would continue to settle his family in the foreign locations he found interesting, despite the prevalence of disease or climates unhealthy for English folk.

Claire Clairmont remained a fixture in their lives. She had produced a lovely child she called Alba, and Shelley busied himself securing recognition of the child by Byron. Though he detested the mother more than ever, Byron readily acknowledged the paternity of Alba and even developed a genuine affection for her. To adequately provide for her daughter's future, Claire reluctantly relinquished her to Byron, as he demanded, though she was to regret this action for the rest of her life. Allegra, as Byron insisted on renaming his little girl, was given over to the care of her father's current mistress. Later, she was committed to a Venetian convent to be reared, and it was there that she died during an epidemic that swept the city. Claire did not hold Byron blameless and nourished her bitter hatred of him from that time forth.

The Shelleys moved to Rome, where the ruins of antiquity inspired them with mournful and noble ideas and provided a picturesque backdrop for their writings. There on June 7, 1819, their remaining child, William, whom they had lovingly called "Wilmouse," died.

Though constantly depressed during this period, Mary was never demobilized by grief. She completed a short novel, *Mathilda*, which she sent to Godwin, expecting him to arrange for its publication. Since its subject was father-daughter incest, it is not surprising that Godwin supressed the manuscript, which was to remain unpublished during Mary's life. From an economic point of view, this was unfortunate, for incest was a titillating topic in the popular fiction of the period, both in England and on the Continent, and the book might have sold well. Aesthetically, it shows little distinction, though biographers have found it useful as a mirror of Mary's mood at the time she wrote it. Her feelings of loneliness, of gloom, and her pervasive sense of having been an inadequate companion to Shelley during this period of grief are all evident. Mary was disappointed that the book did not reach its intended public and probably never realized how uncomfortably it reflected her own attitudes toward both her father and husband.

November 12, 1819, was a happy day in the lives of the Shelleys. They had comfortably settled in pleasing quarters in Florence, in a building across from what is now the central railway station. There Mary gave birth to her only child who was to survive to adulthood and even outlive her. Percy Florence was appropriately named for both his father and his birthplace, the City of Flowers. Sturdy and unexceptional in childhood, he would grow up to be a conventional, thoroughly-reliable citizen. Without either his father's genius or his erratic temperament, Percy Florence was destined for a quiet life as an English gentleman and would become the comfort of his mother's middle age.

Despite her joy in the childhood of Percy Florence, Mary was soon to experience the saddest period of her life. On June 16, 1822, she suffered so painful and dangerous a miscarriage that Claire and Shelley, who attended her, feared for her life. Though she had seen her children come and go and though she well knew the fragility of human life, Mary was still not prepared for the tragedy that struck less than a month later, the loss of Shelley himself.

Shelley had long loved the sea and been ready to sail in any sort of weather. Yet he had never learned to swim. There had been near accidents before, and Mary had warned him of her own premonitions of disaster. On July 8, Shelley and his friends Edward Williams and Charles Vivian made their final excursion. They disappeared during a squall in the Gulf of Spezia, about ten miles west of Viareggio. Ten days after the storm subsided, their mangled bodies were washed ashore. Shelley's remains were cremated on the beach, with local fishermen, Tuscan officials, and friends Leigh Hunt and Lord Byron in mourning. His ashes were taken to the Protestant Cemetery in Rome.

WIDOWHOOD

Mary's poem "The Choice" was written shortly after Shelley's burial. Though devoid of genuine poetic merit, it is a strong personal statement, revealing both the weight of her grief and her sense of guilt. Her loss was to be expressed for the rest of her life. Even though she was scarcely twenty-five years old, she felt that her creative prime was over. Henceforth—and perhaps here she made her chief mistake as a literary artist—she vowed to devote herself to the task of assuring her husband's rightful place in English literature, giving her own talents secondary consideration.

Sir Timothy Shelley still viewed his son as a family embarrassment and feared even further notoriety. It was, sadly, essential that Mary defer to the old gentleman's feelings and whims, refraining during his life from publishing many of the writings commemorating Shelley, which she earnestly desired to see in print. Any misstep threatened a small allowance from Sir Timothy which was essential to Percy Florence's maintenance. Because the elder Shelley never accepted Mary or made provision for her, it was necessary that she continue writing for her own livelihood. After her authorship of *Frankenstein* had been revealed, she had become so well known that there were some who regarded her as a major novelist who was the widow of a minor poet.

Pretending not to take her own literary efforts too seriously, Mary justified them as a means of gaining funds to sustain her genteel poverty and properly educate her son. With minimal help from Sir Timothy, who offered full support of Percy Florence only if Mary would relinquish custody of the boy to him, she nevertheless managed to send her son to the best British schools, patterning his education after that of Lord Byron.

In memory, Shelley the man was quickly idealized, while his poetic powers, to Mary's mind, assumed Shakespearean dimensions. Old hurts and wrongs, when recollected, now appeared to Mary to have been largely her own fault. Certainly Shelley's deep love for her had never been in question. It was easy to forget the problems of their union, especially since she was now reconciled to her father. Though she was still a young woman who might have been expected to remarry, there were no serious romances after Shelley's death, only warm friendships, an occasional emotional exchange of letters, and a few mild flirtations. Mary contended that Shelley was an impossible man to replace, and sometimes she even joked that the name "Shelley" was too euphonious to give up.

A more genuine explanation may have been that she had found marriage more trying than she could bring herself to admit, and the loss of too many children may have left her predisposed to celibacy for the rest of her life. Washington Irving, an author fashionable in England, who moved in the highest literary circles and cut a glamorous, exotic figure as an American, appears to have been the only man she might have considered accepting as a serious suitor. Mary appears to have hinted to friends that she regarded the American author as one whose high character and quality of mind would have made him a worthy successor to Shelley. (4) Though approaches were made to him on her behalf, Irving showed no inclination to come courting. Prosper Merimée the famous French author of *Carmen* and other tales of exotic and violent adventure, appears to have actually proposed marriage. He was refused, despite the likelihood that Mary could have led a stimulating and productive life with this other gifted man of letters.

In addition to supplementing Sir Timothy's slim financial contribution by her literary efforts, Mary had to continue working to contribute funds to Godwin's household. This necessitated a steady schedule of writing. In February of 1823, she published *Valperga*, a historical romance based on Italian lore. Mary's edition of Shelley's *Posthumous Poems* was published in June of 1824, but Sir Timothy strenuously objected and threatened reprisals if the remaining volumes of the edition were not suppressed. Mary reluctantly was forced to comply, after only about three hundred copies had been sold. In 1826 she published her second most significant work of fiction, *The Last Man*. Though too long and excessively verbose by contemporary standards, this powerful apocalyptic novel would become another genuine contribution to science fiction, the genre she is often credited with originating.

Mary was much grieved in 1824 when Lord Byron perished

fighting for Greek independence. Another important link with th
past and the Shelley circle of Geneva was gone. Byron had some
times been a good friend, and Mary had been one of the few wome
he had genuinely admired. His personality had also captured he
literary imagination, as it had that of so many novelists an
poets of the period.

It was a period of high youth mortality. Charles Byssh
Shelley, Shelley's son by Harriet, died in 1826, leaving Perc
Florence heir to the family title and estate, though he was nc
to possess them until his grandfather's death many years later.

Living for a time in Paris in 1828, Mary contracted th
dreaded disease of smallpox. Fortunately her case was light, an
she recovered fully without being disfigured. Still an attrac
tive woman, she was well received in French literary circles an
was even feted by many persons of influence.

Her writings of the next years included *Perkin Warbeck*,
romance based on English history; *Lodore*, often regarded 'as
roman á chef; and biographies written for the Reverend Dionysiu
Lardner's *Cabinet Cyclopedia*. Mary received financial renumera
tion, ample recognition, and considerable satisfaction from he
work for the *Cyclopedia*. Her edition of Shelley's *Poetical Work*
was eventually published in four volumes in 1839, with a second
expanded edition in one volume appearing the following year. Tw
years later she published her edition of *Letters from Abroa*
Translations and Fragments.

As a writer and widow of note, Mary did not escape unwante
attentions. She was the target of a blackmail attempt by a ma
who called himself "Major Byron," and by a literary forger als
tried to prey upon her, but she demonstrated considerable wisdor
and survival skills in dealing with the vultures hovering aroun
her.

Sir Timothy Shelley finally died in 1844, at the age o
ninety-one. Percy Florence became a baron, inheriting resource
that enabled him to live the rest of his life comfortably as
country gentleman. Mary was at last liberated to publish wha
she wished about Shelley. By this time Godwin also had died an
Mary, as his literary executor, could i se his last writing
which, because of their atheism, she had ween reluctant to pub
lish during Sir Timothy's life.

Percy Florence, who doted on his mother, married a woma
much to her taste, Jane St. John, a widow who shared an attach
ment to the memory of Shelley. The new Lady Shelley assiste
Mary in her editing and maintained in her home a library-shrin
to the father-in-law she had never known.

Ianthe, Shelley's surviving child by Harriet, made a suitable marriage to Edward Jeffries Esdaile, a member of a prosper-
ous banking family. While she appears to have experienced some
pride in her father's growing fame, she never joined the circl
of Percy Florence and did not participate in the Shelley cult.

Mary died in London on February 1, 1851, aged fifty-four, after an extended illness and several final days in a coma. Most literary historians have pronounced her life successful, if sad. She was the widow of a great man she had loved; she had almost singlehandedly reared a fine son who was a delight to her in her last years; and she died attended by a daughter-in-law who idolized her. She had contributed substantially to the posthumous fame of her husband, and her own writings had been well received.

Yet the lone facts of a person's life do not really convey the quality of that person's existence. Mary had been frequently described as strong willed, and there were some who knew her in later life who agreed with her father that she was indeed "imperious." She could not always keep old friends, and, after Shelley's death, she complained constantly of betrayals. She may have been a smotheringly-devoted daughter, wife, and mother. There was perhaps some of Wollstonecraft's own masochism in her almost-total self-abnegation, at every stage of her life, to the man who happened to be central at that point, whether father, husband, or son. Though she valiantly worked to secure a pension of the widowed Mrs. Godwin, her words about that aggressive yet struggling stepmother were generally lacking in charity. And Claire Clairmont, too, that acknowledged bane of her existence, may not have been given the full understanding required for a less gifted, envious little stepsister who tried vicariously to experience through Mary a life of love and art. (5)

In sum, Mary Shelley was an admirable woman, but she was not a saint.

Despite the biographical books and essays that have been written about her, there is a general feeling among those who have worked with the materials of her life that Mary is still relatively unknown. Muriel Spark, a fine fiction writer herself, expressed, with some irony, the state of Mary Shelley studies she found a few years ago when she researched her book, *Child of Light: A Reassessment of Mary Wollstonecraft Shelley*:

> Mary Shelley has called forth comparatively little fame—much less, indeed, than her highly entertaining life story and her considerable talent might have been expected to attract. But I do not think this is merely because she has been labelled renegade: but because Shelley's peculiarly white-hot genius has eclipsed her own lambency in posterity's gaze. Apart from being Shelley's wife, she is not confirmed as a character in her own right by any personal myth such as marks other women writers and wives of literary men in our consciousness....Jane Carlyle was a fascinating shrew; Charlotte Bronte, a brave little person; Jane Austen kept her secret; Fanny Brawne was somewhat silly; Aphra Behn, a bad one; Mrs. Gaskell knew everyone; and Elizabeth Barrett Browning came from Wimpole Street. (6)

It might well be added that it is Mary's work rather than her life which has achieved the status of myth. She was no Lord Byron, personally capturing the public imagination, and many do not even associate her name with the myth she originated. Despite the dedication of generations of English teachers, most English-speaking people would be hard pressed to come up with the title of a single poem by Percy Bysshe Shelley. Yet it would be difficult to find any person over the age of six who does not have some response to the name "Frankenstein."

NOTES

1. Ferdinand Lundberg and Marynia Farnham, "Mary Wollstonecraft and the Psychopathology of Feminism," in *A Vindication of the Rights of Woman*, ed. Carol H. Poston, Norton Critical Edition (New York: W.W. Norton Co., 1975), p. 226.

2. Barbara H. Solomon and Paula S. Berggren, eds., *A Wollstonecraft Reader* (New York: New American Library, 1983), p. 265.

3. Frederick L. Jones, ed., *The Letters of Percy Bysshe Shelley* (Oxford: Oxford University Press, 1964), I, 327n. Quoted in William Walling, *Mary Shelley* (Boston: Twayne Publishers, 1972), p. 13

4. Sylva Norman, *The Flight of the Skylark; The Development of Shelley's Reputation* (Norman: University of Oklahoma Press, 1954), p. 66.

5. For a full account of Mary's relationship with her stepsister, see Richard Holmes, *Shelley: The Pursuit* (New York: E.P. Dutton and Co., 1975).

6. Muriel Spark, *Child of Light; A Reassessment of Mary Wollstonecraft Shelley* (Hadleigh: Tower Bridge Publications, 1957), p. 7.

IV
FRANKENSTEIN:
THE BOOK AND ITS RECEPTION

PREFACES AND PLOT

If she had not written *Frankenstein*, Mary Shelley would be remembered only as the wife of an English poet, a woman who did a bit of scribbling on her own. As it is, she may well have written the most influential minor novel of all time in any language. Certainly, she produced one of the most challenging of stories. There seems no end in sight to the books and essays, produced by people of different orientations and vocations, offering "the true meaning" of *Frankenstein* or promising to explore more fully the subterranean depths of the narrative.

Upon its publication, the book enjoyed almost immediate popularity. It was not long before a theatrical adaptation provided a thrilling entertainment on the London stage. After initially publishing the work anonymously and timidly, Mary personally came forth to savor her success, and she seems especially to have enjoyed the stage play. Soon she was taking pleasure in discussing the circumstances of composition. Not only did she experience an author's customary joy in discussing the genesis of an original literary idea, but, in later years, reminiscence became one of her favorite modes of thought, as the genius and saintliness of Shelley grew in her widow's imagination. Shelley's encouragement and the excitement of his presence had been essential to the making of *Frankenstein*.

Memories, notoriously unreliable as the years pass, become especially suspect when they are literary reminiscences, polished for public consumption. Mary was not the only member of the Shelley circle in Geneva who kept journals, and discrepancies between her public recollections and the reporting of others have already been mentioned. Nevertheless, her rationale for composition and her general outline of events are authentic. Because her account benefits from later reflection, it may have a stronger poetic honesty than the more factually correct reports made immediately after the events.

There are two texts of *Frankenstein* from Mary's own pen, issued in 1818 and 1831 respectively. The 1831 edition, which appeared in response to strong popular demand, is less notable for its modest textual revisions than for its "Author's Introductions" in which Mary gives her vivid account of the origin of her tale and her reasons for writing it. Mary claims that she decided to explain herself because her publishers and, no doubt, many readers had often speculated aloud as to how such a young person as herself could have come upon "so very hideous an idea. She proceeds to relate how even as a child, keenly aware of being the daughter of "two persons of distinguished literary celebrity," she had longed to follow family tradition. While growing up, she had "scribbled" diligently, always daydreaming, particularly during that period when she lived in "dark and dreary regions of Scotland which, surprisingly, had never seemed actually melancholy but had appealed to her imagination as places of romance and freedom. Not only had she been inspired to write by the accomplishments of her parents; her husband, too, she acknowledges, had been anxious for her to prove herself worthy of he "parentage" and "enrol herself on the pages of fame." Though she had daydreamed as a child of becoming a famous writer, Mary now piously declares herself, whether honestly or otherwise, indifferent to the worldly glitter. While she was composing *Frankenstein*, there had clearly been other goals and many distractions from the path to celebrity. "Traveling and the cares of a family occupied my time; and study, in the way of reading and improving my ideas in communication with his [Shelley's] far more cultivated mind was all the literary employment that engaged my attention," she modestly says of that period of her life. (1)

In the summer of 1816, her introduction goes on to relate she settled with Shelley in Geneva where they cultivated the friendship of Lord Byron. Together the party wandered the shore. of the lake; enchanted by the scenic beauty of Switzerland After a period of glorious weather, the rains set in, driving them indoors, where they entertained themselves by sharing some German ghost stories that had come their way. Intrigued by Gothic fantasy and looking for a suitable activity until the weather cleared, Lord Byron proposed that they each write a ghost story. "Poor Polidori," as Mary patronizingly refers to Byron's companion and personal physician, concocted the tale which Mary makes light of in her introduction but which, in fact, is still anthologized and regarded as a classic early vampire story.

Byron started his own tale with enthusiasm but, after producing only a fragment, lost interest. Shelley's mind, seemingly, proved to be too fine for such crudities. Mary recalls that "Shelley, more apt to embody ideas and sentiments in the radiance of brilliant imagery and in the music of the most melodious verse that adorns our language than to invent the machinery of a story, commenced one founded on the experiences of his early life." (2) Those who knew Shelley were well aware of his tendency to recast his childhood in fearful and heroic scenarios, yet he too appears never to have finished his tale.

Though she may have renounced the vain pride of literary fame, the conclusion to Mary's introduction clearly demonstrates her joy of authorship, her sense of achievement in reaching a wide, enthusiastic audience, and her genuine affection for *Frankenstein*:

34

And now, once again, I bid my hideous progeny go forth and prosper. I have an affection for it, for it was the offspring of happy days, when death and grief were but words which found no true echo in my heart. Its several pages speak of many a walk, many a drive, and many a conversation when I was not alone; and my companion was he who, in this world, I shall never see more. But this is for myself; my readers have nothing to do with these associations. (3)

In reality, as all readers of biographies of the Shelleys know, those days now remembered so fondly were by no means as free of death and sorrow as she seems to suggest in retrospect. The *Frankenstein* period was actually a trying time for all members of the Geneva circle.

In her introduction, Mary also comments on most of the textual changes she made in her 1831 revision. They are, on the whole, without great significance, and many of her readers have always preferred the earlier version, which they feel embodies more classically and honestly her initial vision. The alterations, according to Mary's own accounting, changed no portion of the basic story and introduced no new ideas or circumstances. She claims to have refined the language to the improvement of her narrative, and most of her changes are to be found only at the beginning of the first volume. The "core and substance," of the story, she strongly affirms, are unchanged. As will be seen, there were more significant changes than Mary cared to mention, for sensitive reasons she preferred not to discuss in print.

The new edition also includes an earlier preface which had originally appeared unsigned but which Mary now reveals to be entirely Shelley's work. His preface, which readers would have accepted as the author's own in the first version, stresses the presumed scientific basis on which the credibility of the narrative rests. He invokes the name of Dr. Erasmus Darwin (the grandfather of the author of *The Origin of the Species*) and some unnamed "physiological writers of Germany" to suggest that the events related in Mary's narrative, peculiar as they might seem, are not outside the realm of possibility. Mary seriously endeavored, he asserts, to preserve "the truth of the elementary principles of human nature," without resorting to the use of supernatural terrors to enhance the suspense of her narrative. Rather pompously, he lists as influences and sources the *Iliad* of Homer, the tragic poetry of Greece, Shakespeare's *The Tempest*, and *A Midsummer Night's Dream*, and, most especially, Milton's *Paradise Lost*. He reminds the reader, perhaps as a protection from harsh judgment, that the circumstances on which the story rests were suggested by casual conversation and the writing was done for amusement and to exercise "untried resources of mind." Yet there are, admittedly, more serious motives also operating. Though it is possibly little more than an attempt to follow the familiar conventions of author's prefaces, Shelley attributes lofty ethical goals to Mary. She has sought, he says, to promote amiable domestic affection and the excellence of universal truth while avoiding the enervating effects of most of the novels o her time.

Challenged by the game Byron proposed that rainy evening Mary had obviously busied herself thinking of a story. The conversations at which she had been an eager-eyed and susceptibl listener had been carefully stored in her memory:

> Many and long were the conversations between Lord Byron and Shelley to which I was a devout but nearly silent listener. During one of these, various philosophical doctrines were discussed, and among others the nature of the principle of life and whether there was any probability of its ever being discovered and communicated. They talked of the experiments of Dr. Darwin (I speak not of what the doctor really did or said that he did, but, as more to my purpose, of what was then spoken of as having been done by him), who preserved a piece of vermicelli in a glass case till by some extraordinary means it began to move with voluntary motion. Not thus, after all, would life be given. Perhaps a corpse would be reanimated, galvanism had given token of such things, perhaps the component parts of a creature might be manufactured, brought together, and endued with vital warmth. (4)

In this way Mary's fertile imagination was stimulated whil she established, at the same time, verisimilitude and a basis o scientific plausibility, however remote, for her tale. Shelley' preface stresses this pseudo-scientific base even more, apparent ly in all seriousness.

In remembering the germination of her tale, Mary speaks o the shadows of night falling on the small but highly-stimulate company around the fireside; as they fought off the damp, sh remembers that they distracted their minds from the physica discomforts with tales of alchemy and witchcraft. Retiring lat after one such conversation, Mary found herself tossing restless ly in her bed, without a coherent train of thought. Her imagina tion wandered in successive images until what she called "a acute mental vision" appeared:

> I saw the pale student of unhallowed arts kneeling beside the thing he had put together. I saw the hideous phantasm of a man stretched out, and then, on the working of some powerful engine, show signs of life and stir with an uneasy half-vital motion. Frightful must it be, for supremely frightful would be the effect of any human endeavour to mock the stupendous mechanism of the Creator of the world. His success would horrify the artist: he would rush away from his odious handiwork, horror-stricken. He would hope that, left to itself, the slight spark of life which he had communi-

cated would fade, that this thing which had received such imperfect animation would subside into dead matter, and he might sleep in the belief that the silence of the grave would quench forever the transient existence of the hideous corpse which he had looked upon as the cradle of life. He sleeps; but he is awakened; he opens his eyes; behold, the horrid thing stands at his bedside, opening his curtains and looking on him with yellow, watery but speculative eyes. (5)

The vision, more real than any daydream, terrified Mary; many strands of the conversations she had heard in recent days and even earlier in the Godwin house in England came together in keen images "in a thrilling sort of fearful way." She appears to have shared her vision almost immediately with Shelley, who urged her to develop it as a narrative and later to expand it from a short story to a full-length novel.

Of Mary's two *Frankenstein* texts, the one of 1831 is today the more frequently published, though foreign translations have been made of both. Leonard Wolf, who has perceptively studied both narratives, feels that the first edition is preferable because it preserves the voice of an eighteen year old "demi-bohemian in the grip of necessity." Fifteen years later, much had changed, and Mary was a well-known writer, the widow of a distinguished man rather than his pregnant *paramour*. Wolf feels the changes in · the second edition reflect less Mary's development as a creative artist than her increased striving for greater social respectability. (6)

Though the changes Mary wrought in her text do not make it any more palatable to contemporary tastes, they are of considerable interest to the student of literature. In what is generally regarded as an attempt to make him more Shelleyesque, Victor Frankenstein is made more handsome and noble than he initially appeared. Walton, the explorer who rescues Victor from the sea and is the auditor for his horrible story, has been fleshed out, supplied with clearer motivations and more "refined sensibilities." Victor's parents, Alphonse and Caroline Frankenstein, have also matured, and their domestic relationships have deepened since 1818. Yet the most significant change is seen in the account of the origins of Elizabeth, Victor's unfortunate bride. In 1818 she was his first cousin, in a relationship bordering on incest. By 1831 Mary, who had smarted from family aversion to *Mathilda*, had made Elizabeth a foundling, though she is discovered to be of aristocratic Milanese blood. She is, therefore, unrelated to Victor, though brought up in his home as both foster sister and intended bride. Readers today have much difficulty understanding the erotic appeal the "boy or girl next door," or even within the same walls, had for the early-nineteenth-century reader, though current erotic literature has made some attempt to revive "my sister, my spouse" as a titillating subject.

Despite the attempts of both Shelleys, in their introductions and in the preface, to stress the grounding of the tale in scientific plausibility rather than German spiritualism or medieval magic, real science plays little role. Victor Frankenstein resembles the Romantic rebel artist more than a scientist, mad or otherwise. Mary appears to have been almost totally ignorant of the scientific explorations of her day, and she makes little effort to give verisimilitude by sprinkling scientific words or laboratory jargon into the conversations of her characters. At points where a science-fiction writer today would go into paragraphs of scientific or pseudo-scientific explanation, Mary simply skims, implies, or ducks the issue altogether. Even her powers of scientific prophecy were severely limited, as can be even more clearly observed in her later novel, *The Last Man*, where she projects a future that is only slightly different from her own time.

Victor Frankenstein is introduced as a chemist and anatomist who has delved into dangerous lore, but there is no evidence that his native gifts or academic training are such as to equip him for the discovery of the origin and creation of life, a secret that has escaped the most learned alchemists, wizards, chemists, and other scientists and occultists, ancient and modern, in either real life or most fiction. The reader must take on faith Victor's overwhelming scientific genius, which, coupled with a few strokes of luck, accounts for his success. After two years of university, working in his private chambers, he accomplishes what the world's leading scientists in the best equipped laboratories would scarcely even attempt.

The outline of the book is quite different from the plots so well known to viewers of the many Frankenstein films. The spectacular windmill laboratory that Universal Studios provided Frankenstein does not appear at all in the novel. Young Frankenstein resembles a clever teenage computer hacker more than an academically-recognized genetic engineer working in facilities generously subsidized by private or public grants.

Because the film scenarios are so well known, it is necessary to reconstruct the Frankenstein story as Mary Shelley herself envisioned it. The tale begins when Walton, an English explorer whose ship is temporarily stranded in polar ice, takes aboard the disheveled Victor Frankenstein, a strange wanderer who has appeared out of the frozen wastes in a weakened condition. During his convalescence, Frankenstein explains to Walton his presence in this desolate region and tells him an almost unbelievable life story. He recounts his birth into a prominent Geneva family, his childhood in a happy home with loving parents, a younger brother, and an adopted little sister. Stung by his mother's premature death during his early manhood, Frankenstein brooded on the nature of life. Having shown early promise in the natural sciences and studied the works of Paracelsus and Albertus Magnus, Victor seemed ready to be sent by his father to the University of Ingolstadt for an orthodox education. Working on the periphery of the university, he sought arcane knowledge and explored scientific techniques which would benefit humanity and prolong life. Obsessed by his discoveries, it was easy to forget his initial benevolent goals when he boldly resolved to construct an artificial human being. Frequenting butcher's shops and dissecting rooms, he was finally able to assemble enough oddly assorted parts for his creation. The result was an eight-foot, grotesquely asymmetrical monster.

Fans of the James Whale films may be disappointed to learn that Frankenstein had no assistant, and there was no criminal brain placed in the monster's skull.

As soon as the creature showed life and his horrible eye opened, Frankenstein was seized by remorse and fled his quarters, thereby deserting the being he had brought to life and refusing to take any responsibility for him. Frankenstein, obviously not up to the task of nurturing the Monster (who quickly develops a personality of his own), revealed himself to be a fragile man who easily faints in a crisis. After the success of his terrible experiment, he developed brain fever but was nursed to recovery by his friend from Geneva, Henry Clerval, who nevertheless learned nothing of the nature of Frankenstein's work.

From Geneva word arrived that Victor's younger brother, William, had been found horribly strangled in a park. A loyal and trusted family servant, Justine, had been apprehended with incriminating evidence found on her person. Knowing in his heart that this crime is the work of his Monster, Victor hastened to Geneva. Elizabeth, his foster sister, who was also certain of Justine's innocence, made an eloquent plea at her trial, but because Victor himself defended her only half-heartedly, Justine was convicted and executed.

To dissipate his depression, Victor absconded to the mountains. On a glacier, one of Mary Shelley's several dramatically atmospheric settings, he came face to face with his Monster, who had now been alive for about a year. In that short time the Monster had learned to speak eloquently and had a story of his own to relate.

In his narrative within a narrative, the Monster told his maker how he had left the chambers where he came to life. His every encounter with humans had quickly caused panic. Wandering in a confused state of dejection, he eventually found shelter in an abandoned hovel next to a cottage inhabited by the DeLacey family. This harmonious family was headed by a blind widowed father. From a hidden vantage point, the Monster was able to follow the lives of the DeLaceys. Eating berries gathered by night and, like a good fairy, aiding the family by chopping wood and performing other unseen tasks, the Monster lived in relative peace. Through his eavesdropping, he learned the French language spoken by the DeLaceys and the meaning of family relationships. By one of several amazing coincidences in the novel, he also found a trunk of well-chosen, excellent books which provided him an unusual education. Since Frankenstein had conveniently left his scientific notebook in the pocket of an old jacket the Monster had taken from his birth chamber, the creature had even come to understand the uniqueness of his origins.

Coincidences truly abound in Mary's novel. The people in

the cottage were not really peasants, it was soon learned, but educated, well-born Parisians who had fallen on unhappy days. The Monster was, thus, fortunately situated to absorb a high level of culture. Longing for friendship, he finally gained enough courage to make himself known to the blind father of the family, but when the other DeLaceys returned home to behold his hideousness, they were stricken by the same fear he had aroused in all other humans he had encountered. They fled in terror.

Thus rejected by the cottagers, the Monster nursed a bitterness toward all humankind. Wandering in a park near Geneva, he came upon William Frankenstein, an insufferable lad who, again coincidentally, just happened to be playing there alone. With a wickedness for which the reader is not fully prepared, the Monster strangled the boy and took from his body a painting of the child's deceased mother, which he then planted on the sleeping servant girl nearby.

After relating to his creator his grim story, the Monster made the terrible demand which was to inspire so many motion picture sequels. He had learned through his reading and by observing the DeLacey family that all creatures have mates. Frankenstein now must fashion for him a female companion, he decreed, with whom he would then retreat to desolate wastes to eke out his years and never trouble human beings again. Though Frankenstein saw some justice in the request and initially agreed to comply, upon later reflection he recoiled with horror at the vision of himself as maker of a hideous race of monsters. Although he did proceed to assemble the parts for the female, as he had promised, working at the terrible task in the remote Orkneys, he could not bring himself to complete the work. In a fit of revulsion and remorse, he destroyed the female when she was near completion. The Monster, who had been watching through a window, was agonized to see his hopes of companionship shattered. Deprived of his own bride, he warned Victor that he would be with him and Elizabeth in vengeance on their wedding night. Escaping by sea, the Monster next killed Victor's faithful friend Henry Clerval in an Existential fury.

Victor returned to Geneva where, despite what had transpired, he went ahead with his marriage plans. Assuming that it was his own life at stake, Victor made suitable arrangements for his defense. After giving Elizabeth a mysterious warning, he left her alone in their nuptial chamber and left to stalk the Monster. However, the reader has already discerned that the creature had more diabolical intentions than Frankenstein imagined. Entering the nuptial chamber through the casement, he fatally strangled Elizabeth. There was to be no happy ending, with Victor and Elizabeth Frankenstein reunited in one another's arms, as in the original Whale film. Widowed on his wedding night, Victor was now filled with complete hatred of his creature, vowing to track him down and destroy him as the last act of his own forlorn life. This episode marked the beginning of an odyssey that would take hunter and prey through the lands of the North, toward the Pole itself, where Victor would encounter Walton, who would hear his woeful tale.

Weakened by his exposure to the harsh Arctic elements and the emotions aroused by relating his narrative, Victor dies attended by Walton, before he can accomplish his mission. To say his last farewell, the Monster enters the ship's cabin where his maker's body rests. Having succeeded in destroying the one who gave him life, he makes a promise to Walton, who has faithfully kept vigil. The Monster foretells his own approaching death on a funeral pyre in the frozen wastes. How he will manage this spectacular end in this unlikely *milieu* and who will provide the wood are not made clear. Yet the Monster vanishes into an ice field, presumably to act upon his promise.

THEMES AND MOTIFS OF FRANKENSTEIN

Females and Feminism

There are features that deserve discussion on every page of Mary Shelley's bizarre and wonderful narrative. Though the characters are little more than stick figures when compared to those which populate nineteenth- and twentieth-century realistic novels, they are sometimes presented in interesting ways. Women occupy a rather peculiar position. Elizabeth's intramural romance is no longer very titillating, and she remains too much the stereotypical heroine of sentimental fiction—lovely, virtuous, and put upon—to evoke much sympathy today. The single point at which she does rise to some stature is the occasion of her impassioned plea for Justine's life. She certainly demonstrates more forceful ethical conduct at every turn than does Victor.

But the characterization of Elizabeth deserves comment for another reason. Mary Shelley, daughter of Wollstonecraft, the quintessential feminist, has presented Elizabeth, in all seeming seriousness, as the ideal bride for young Frankenstein and a woman for the reader to admire. Yet Elizabeth is far from being a self-realized woman, even by the standards of the popular fiction of her day. She is intelligent, to be sure, but always docile. It is without question—or even second thought—that she has accepted the family decree of her marriage to Victor. Duty and humility are her dominant traits: no matter how illustrious her birth, she never forgets that she is a rescued orphan who owes the Frankenstein family the full commitment of her life.

Mrs. Frankenstein, mother of the scientist, is another withering, idealized woman of the early-nineteenth-century romance. Fragile women were in fashion, and a semi-invalid wife was regarded as a status symbol of a wealthy man, who could afford servants to maintain his house and attend his spouse. Mrs. Frankenstein's deathbed prophecies, wishes, and promises, foreshadowing later events and recapitulating earlier ones, are another familiar feature of the sentimental literature of the period. Every dramatic trapping is present at her death except descending angels to carry her soul to paradise. It is hard to resist the temptation to compare her calm and dignified fictional death with the tortured reality of Wollstonecraft's death in childbed, Wollstonecraft's physical pain, complicated by the indignities of the medical treatments of the time. If Mary felt any irony, she did not reveal it.

Safie, the bride of the cottager, Felix DeLacey, is the character who best approximates the free woman envisioned by the writing of Wollstonecraft. As the eavesdropping Monster soon learns, Safie was born in Turkey, the daughter of a Moslem father by a captive Christian-European mother, from whom she absorbed ideals of freedom and views of marriage as a loving equal companionship. When Safie escaped from her father's house and the future of harem life he had planned for her, she asserted her independence. She chose to be the bride and educated equal of a European.

Education

Both Mary's parents developed strongly pronounced theories of education, and it is not surprising that Mary would give some attention to patterns of education for her principle characters. Young Frankenstein's education remarkably resembles Mary's own program of self-instruction, which she outlined in some detail in her journal. It is clear that she embarked on an ambitious plan of reading during the Geneva period. John Milton was much on her mind at this time, as she visited almost daily Villa Diodata, the residence of Lord Byron in which it was claimed Milton had lived. Mary probably knew of the extraordinary regimen of self-education outlined and indeed executed by the great English epic poet. Keenly feeling her inferiority to Shelley in general culture, she may have, in her more modest way, tried to emulate Milton. Like him, she was particularly keen on foreign languages, and she sought to read widely in the literature of all countries and periods. In her book, she allows young Frankenstein to follow a comparable plan. At an early age he studies mathematics and related disciplines, along with languages. Having mastered Latin, he begins reading the easiest Greek authors without the help of a lexicon. His English and German comprehension is soon perfect. He is, of course, already articulate in his native tongue, French. Thus, by the age of seventeen, Frankenstein is already a man of wide culture.

Ambitious though Frankenstein's program of study was, it is the Monster's education that leaves the reader gasping in wonder! During their second meeting, the Monster explains to Frankenstein, who failed in what was certainly his primary duty to nurture and instruct him, how he learned to talk by observing and listening to the DeLacey family. And he was indeed a fast learner, a gifted child-man, the most remarkable self-made individual on record in reality or fiction. Fortuitiously, the DeLaceys had the task of teaching Safie, the young Turkish bride, how to speak

French and, by listening, the Monster was able to learn along with her.

Leonard Wolf, tongue in cheek, has compared the Monster's linguistic feats to those of Edgar Rice Burroughs' hero, Tarzan, who by examining discarded English books in the middle of the African jungle taught himself to read.

Felix DeLacey, a teacher of some discernment, instructs Safie from Volney's *Ruins of Empires*, while the Monster listens. An instinctive and passionate lover of liberty, who would have warmed the heart of Godwin, the Monster immediately becomes an ardent supporter of the French Revolution, an advocate of the Enlightenment, and even the champion of Native American Indians! In his own words, tinged with a European chauvinism no doubt also learned from the DeLaceys, he interprets Felix's lessons for Safie:

> Through this work [*Ruins of Empire*] I obtained a cursory knowledge of history, and a view of the several empires at present existing in the world; it gave me an insight into the manners, governments, and religions of the different nations of the earth. I heard of the slothful Asiatics; of the stupendous genius and mental activity of the Grecians; of the wars and wonderful virtue of the early Romans—and of their subsequent degeneration—of the decline of that mighty empire; of chivalry, Christianity, and kings. I heard of the discovery of the American hemisphere, and wept with Safie over the hapless fate of its original inhabitants. (7)

It is, however, the reading material which the Monster finds in an abandoned trunk that influences him most. It molds his thought and provides Mary with some meager justification for articulating in this book several of her own favorite themes. The books in the leather *portmanteau* had been carefully selected by some unknown person. Each volume adds another dimension to the Monster's education and consequently to the development of his attitude toward the agonies of his existence. The books are *The Sorrows of Young Werther*, Goethe's tale of the ecstasy and pain of love, which suggests suicide as a suitable remedy for the sickness; Plutarch's *Parallel Lives*, which from antiquity has taught that the lives of public men, for good and ill, are exempla; and, most significantly of all, John Milton's epic poem *Paradise Lost*, which relates divine events of which the Monster's own creation seems a cruel and grotesque parody. Though Milton may not have fully succeeded in his stated goal of justifying God's ways to man, his writing brilliantly clarified for the Monster his own plight. No loved and blessed Adam, coddled by his Creator and given every good gift, the rejected Monster identifies with Satan—that Miltonic figure of solemn majesty which so intrigued the English Romantic Movement—and takes evil for his good.

Though there is no mention of the Monster's having had the benefits of exposure to Shelley's poetry, he does paraphrase "Mutability" at one point. He is certainly, in his best moments, embued with a Shelleyan sensibility, and on one notable occasion he even comes out in support of Shelley's doctrine of vegetarianism. "My food is not that of man," he somewhat sanctimoniously tells Frankenstein. "I do not destroy the lamb and the kid, to glut my appetite; acorns and berries afford me sufficient nourishment." (8)

It is *Paradise Lost*, however, which most thoroughly captures the Monster's imagination:

> I read it, as I had read the other volumes which had fallen into my hands, as a true history. It moved every feeling of wonder and awe, that the picture of an omnipotent God warring with his creatures was capable of exciting.
> I often referred to the several situations, as their similarity struck me, to my own. Like Adam, I was created apparently united by no link to any other being in existence; but his state was far different from mine in every other respect. He had come forth from the hands of God a perfect creature, happy and prosperous, guarded by the especial care of his Creator; he was allowed to converse with, and acquire knowledge from beings of a superior nature; but I was wretched, helpless, and alone. (9)

The Monster views his lot as even more miserable than that of Milton's Satan, who at least had companions in damnation, fellow-devils who shared his wickedness in that dark kingdom where he reigned in sinister splendor. Alone of all creatures, Frankenstein's Monster sees himself as totally solitary and detested by all beings, good or evil. This solitary desolation is the prevailing mood of the book.

Having read his Milton so carefully, the Monster knows that God Almighty, more thoughtful in all ways than Victor Frankenstein, quickly provided his Adam with a mate. Realizing that it is not good for either man or Monster to be alone, the creature approaches Frankenstein with that proposal both reasonable and horrible—he too deserves a mate:

> Remember thou hast made me more powerful than thy self; my height is superior to thine; my joints more supple. But I will not be tempted to set myself in opposition to thee. I am thy creature, and I will be even mild and docile to my natural lord and king, if thou wilt also perform thy part, the which thou owest me. Oh, Frankenstein, be not equitable to every other, and trample upon me alone, to whom thy justice, and even thy clemency and affection is most due. Remember, that I am thy creature; I ought to be thy Adam; but I am

rather the fallen angel, whom thou drivest from joy for
no misdeed. Every where I see bliss, from which I
alone am irrevocably excluded. I was benevolent and
good; misery made me a fiend. Make me happy, and I
shall again be virtuous. (10)

It is to be noted that, in addressing his maker, the Monster, always subtle, uses the archaic linguistic mode of prayer
and supplication.

Despite his wretchedness, the Monster rejects suicide. Like
the ancient Greek and Roman Stoics, the troubled protagonists of
the Gothic novel frequently availed themselves of the "open door"
of suicide. In the sentimental novel death was, in fact, sometimes as ardently sought as a lover's embrace. Goethe's *The
Sorrows of Young Werther* made suicide fashionable and inspired a
wave of suicides throughout Europe. Life imitates art just as
art imitates life; suicides, both abortive and realized, had
already touched Mary and would touch her again. Both Frankenstein
and the Monster, at different times, contemplate suicide and then
provide their reasons for rejecting it, as if the choice to
continue life needed a defense. Only in the final fatal act
promised by the Monster, if we are to believe it did indeed
occur, is a calm form of self-destruction chosen on the Polar
ice.

Religious Themes and Issues

The anti-religious and anti-clerical sentiments Mary learned
in the Godwin parlor occasionally slip into her narrative. Cler-
gymen are probably more absent than they would have been in real
life in a segment of Genevan society comparable to Mary's fictional *milieu.* When a priest does appear to attend Justine in
the hours before her execution, he is shown in an unfavorable
light. He hectors her, forcing a perjurous confession from her
lips, thus behaving in a manner which, were he real rather than
fictional, would get him defrocked.

Mary's own religious views have been subject to some discussion. While Godwin's atheism is well known and while Shelley's
unbelief was probably the major point of contention between him
and his own father, Sir Timothy, it is not absolutely clear to
what extent Mary accepted the views of her father and husband.
There are some hints in both her commercial and personal writings
that she was not totally untouched by the conventional, sentimental piety of her age. It is likely that she never developed
either a consistent theological or anti-theological position.
She certainly spoke several times of her hope of being reunited
with Shelley after death on some higher plane, but even Shelley's
own atheism did not necessarily preclude the possibility of
ghosts, reincarnation, and other spiritual phenomena.

It is always precarious, in the pursuit of information, to
attribute beliefs and sentiments of fictional characters to their

authors. Yet *Frankenstein* is in many ways, more than most romances, a personal statement. In the novel "wandering spirits" are sometimes invoked. However, neither Victor nor his Monster ever calls upon God directly. Elizabeth indeed uses God's name, but as the sentimental heroine she would be expected to harbor conventionally pious feelings, and even she never addresses God directly in prayer. Though Mary Shelley appears reluctant to exclude a spiritual dimension from her narrative or the lives of her characters, they are allowed no real comfort from either the Christian or the Deistic God. The Monster, in one of the several graceful little moments of the narrative, takes an oath on Frankenstein's name, the name of his own maker. "I swear to you," he says, "by the earth which I inhabit, and by you that made me, that, with the companion you bestow, I will quit the neighbourhood of man, and dwell, as it may chance, in the most savage of places." (11)

There is also, permeating the story, the inescapable awareness that Frankenstein in creating life has infringed on the prerogatives of some Higher Power and is certain to experience retribution.

Mary's novel, more than any film it has inspired, demands to be read in part as a theological parable. The Monster has interpreted his own existence through his reading of *Paradise Lost*. His relationship with Frankenstein reflects in its crude way the struggle between the Hebrew God and the Biblical patriarchs. Denounced by his creator in the most abusive language, the Monster reminds Frankenstein that it is bad potters who make inferior pots.

Significantly, the creature is never given a name. He is merely Frankenstein's Monster, though viewers of the films, and later on even the film scripts themselves, will give the Monster his maker's name. Yet in the book, Frankenstein has so little regard for the living work of his hands that he never bestows on him a name, even as one would to a domestic animal. "Nobody knows my name" is the anguished perpetual cry of the rejected of the Earth, and perhaps the Bible's most terrifying threat is that God Almighty will blot the names of the wicked from the Book of Life and remember them no more.

Frankenstein, though a slow learner, gradually comes to acknowledge that the creator does have some duties to his creature. In temporarily acceding to the Monster's demand for a mate, it does occur to him that the female may well reject the Monster, finding him as hideous as do humans. She may even prefer the association of mankind, particularly if she, as the second and improved work, is more gracefully constructed. The films were later to fully exploit these suggested possibilities, much too tantalizing to be left alone. Today numerous students of cinema history prefer James Whale's *Bride of Frankenstein*, with the handsome, hissing Elsa Lancaster as the Monsteress, to *Frankenstein* itself.

46

Family Relationships

The Monster's observations of family relationships—the difference between the sexes, the birth and nurture of children, the love of parents, the concern, especially, of mother for child—reveal his own isolation even more totally. That *Frankenstein* is peculiarly a book of male parents has not escaped notice. There are many fathers but no truly present mothers. The Monster comes to life in full height and proportion, motherless and begotten, as it were, only by Frankenstein, without female assistance. Frankenstein's own ethereal mother dies early on. Justine's mother has rejected her in childhood, and Elizabeth, too, is an orphan. In the DeLacey cottage, a patriarch benevolently provides for the family, while again there is no mother. Safie, the reader is told, also lost her mother in childhood, and with the murder of Frankenstein's bride another potential mother of children is disposed of. Mary, probably without consciously realizing it, filled this book with her own aching sense of maternal deprivation, for she too could never erase from mind the fact that she had been reared by a father. Some psychoanalytic interpreters of the novel have read it as an even more troubling statement of Mary's revulsion against her own experiences of maternity.

Sexuality

Though *Frankenstein* is devoid of overt sexuality, there is a persistent undertone of dark sensuality, and the erotically-charged atmosphere will be recognized by any habitual reader of Gothic romance. The undercurrent of sexual violence is all the more powerful for being implied rather than rendered explicit. The Monster is eye-witness to the entire lives of the DeLacey family, observing with mounting excitement Felix's courtship of Safie. The pattern of voyeurism established at the DeLacey cottage continues as the Monster, through a window, observes Frankenstein at work on the promised mate. It reaches its culmination in Frankenstein's wedding chamber, with the Monster peering at the bride through the casement and later entering the room for his own violent consummation of Frankenstein's nuptuals. The *fleur de mal* decadence of these scenes was well captured by some of the early illustrators of editions of the book, and it is not really surprising that later novelists reworking the materials have sometimes added monster copulations and scenes of both soft and hardcore pornography. The Monster's longing for a mate is certainly sexual, even while it stems from his utter loneliness and rejection by all mankind. In describing his wrath when he sees Victor Frankenstein destroy the monsteress, Mary was able to imply the erotic frustration and violence she could not describe directly.

A major Godwinian theme had been reinforced by Mary's readings of Jean-Jacques Rousseau. The Monster is presented as having been essentially innocent and good at his moment of creation. The will to do evil enters his heart only after the world rejects him and heaps its prejudice and irrationality on his head. His primordial innocence is corrupted more and more by each human encounter, beginning with Frankenstein himself. It is quite clear that Victor is at fault as much for abandoning and rejecting his creature as for usurping divine perogatives in making him in the first place.

Had his natural inclinations not been perverted, we are led to believe that the Monster would have demonstrated a remarkable social consciousness. As he listens to the conversations of the DeLacey family, he shudders to hear of the oppression of women in Moslem harems. Of course, he cannot have known that this description of harem captivity was taken from the stories of Wollstonecrft and did not much resemble actual Turkish family life at the time, though it reflected the belief of the British and most Europeans that the Turks were the great badmen of the world.

The Monster's conversation reveals him to be innately a being of the Enlightenment. Always a perceptive listener and reader, he has meditated on both the magnificence and the viciousness of mankind. From the cottagers, he has received an introduction to economics that could have come from William Godwin himself, learning how property has been unfairly divided so that immense wealth exists side by side with squalid poverty. From them, he has also learned of the abuses of rank, descent, and noble blood. Yet seeing the importance humans place on family ties and lineage only makes him feel his unique freakishness the more keenly.

The Monster understands all too clearly why Rousseau and Godwin spoke of "the warped values of men." He sees that, in view of these values, he will always be despised, possessing no lineage, money, friends, or property, and endowed with a hideous and deformed body. He sees that he is scarcely of the same nature as men, stronger and larger in stature than they, more agile and able to subsist on a coarser diet, possessing a body more easily bearing the extremes of heat and cold. Yet, rather than viewing himself as a superman, the Monster calls himself "a blot on the earth." Excluded from human society, which he longs to enter despite its inequities, he learns another lesson from *Paradise Lost*; he takes evil as his good and determines to outdo even the wickedness of men, patterning his actions on those of Milton's Satan.

Scenic Qualities

Though the films were later to dwarf the book in scenic impact, Mary demonstrated considerable skill in composing scenes for the mind's eye of her reader. Admittedly Frankenstein's student quarters, where the Monster comes to life, cannot compare with the windmill laboratory, replete with mysterious machines and gadgets, provided by Universal Studios. Yet the book provides a few grand set pieces which the cinema did not attempt to reproduce. The desolate glacier on which Frankenstein meets his Monster is one example, and the frozen North into which Frankenstein pursues his Monster is another. Geneva itself is a city of picturesque charm. Mary's characters are, further, constantly on the move. They travel quickly from Switzerland, up the Rhine, through England, Scotland, Russia and on to regions beyond. Unlike his lumbering cinema counterpart, Mary's Monster moves quickly and efficiently through dramatic geography.

Intensifying the visual quality of the book's locales is the full co-operation of nature in the climactic fictional moments. Nowhere is this more clearly demonstrated than in the account of Frankenstein's wedding night. There is a heavy rain storm and nature provides fireworks appropriate to either an erotic consummation or a thanatopsis. Elizabeth in death is thrown across her bed, that bridal bier, in a classic scene of Gothic eroticism. From the casement, the Monster grins at his handiwork.

Doppelgänger and Aristotelian Hero

For the fans of both the old and new Frankenstein movies, the book's subdued account of the Monster's coming-to-life is initially a disappointment, though it is actually a highly skilled passage of suspense writing:

> It was on a dreary night of November, that I beheld the accomplishment of my toils. With an anxiety that almost amounted to agony, I collected the instruments of life around me, that I might infuse a spark of being into the lifeless thing that lay at my feet. It was already one in the morning; the rain pattered dismally against the panes, and my candle was nearly burnt out, when, by the glimmer of the half-extinguished light, I saw the dull yellow eye of the creature open; it breathed hard, and a convulsive motion agitated its limbs. (12)

Frankenstein faints at this moment, just as he collapses during each major crisis throughout the book. His own age might have described this manner of withdrawal from unpleasant situations as "sensitive"; our generation will be less kind to fictional heroes such as Werther and Frankenstein. Yet in this pattern of behavior, as in others, Frankenstein resembles Shelley, who is known to have experienced seizures. Frankenstein endures periods of delirum, which come with more frequency as his distress mounts. It is almost certain that Mary regarded such conduct, in both her husband and her fictional hero, as a mark of heightened sensibility rather than a lack of manliness. The reader was intended to visualize a thin, poetically romantic man against glaciers and dark clouds.

Though Victor Frankenstein does not impress the contemporary reader with his insight, he does appear to possess a dim awareness that the Monster is a dark shadow of himself. The Monster stalks him, watches him from casements, constantly crosses his path, and even steps into his place for a bloody wedding night ritual. The Monster is clearly a *doppelgänger*, another sinister figure from the German horror story that became familiar to all European literature during the period.

This terrible shadow, or double, haunts the entire Frankenstein family, though only Victor understands why all the people near him seem cursed. William, Elizabeth, and Justine are destroyed. Clerval is also murdered. Victor's father dies of grief, and Victor himself bcomes a wanderer. He is the Romantic exile, another fictional type of the period, fleeing his double yet always accompanied by him wherever he goes. Though not constantly in view of one another, Victor and the creature seem propelled by the same forces in their wanderings. At one point they arrive simultaneously in Russia. When Victor makes his vow to destroy the Monster, he knows from unseen laughter that he has been overheard by his intended victim.

Mary attempted to give young Victor some of the qualities of an Aristotelian hero as well as those of a doomed Romantic exile. He speaks of his youthful intimations of destiny, how he felt himself called to great enterprises, entrusted with talents to be used to benefit fellow creatures. Yet young Frankenstein is one whose great talents and noble aspirations have led to disaster through a fatal flaw in his nature, the pride of the overreacher. At the end he has come to believe that Heaven itself demands that he work out his terrible destiny, the destruction of the Monster and himself in the process.

To make the Aristotelian message even more unmistakable, the dying Frankenstein—who is expiring from exposure without really fulfilling his vow to destroy the Monster—warns Walton of the dangers of pride: "Seek happiness in tranquillity, and avoid ambition, even if it be only the apparently innocent one of distinguishing yourself in science and discoveries." (13)

It is from Walton that the reader receives the best description of the Monster, in a scene which reinforces the *doppelganger* motif and reveals again the love-hate relationship between Frankenstein and his creature. The Monster, like man, has learned the bitter comforts of guilt and now leaps to take responsibility for his maker's death, acknowledging that he has committed a form of parricide-deicide. It does not really matter that Frankenstein died from exposure and not actually by the Monster's hand. The creature's grief is genuine. Without Frankenstein to hate, there is no longer any reason for his own continued existence. More clearly than any other action or words previously uttered, the Monster's speech over Frankenstein's corpse reveals the love-hate bond which has motivated him:

...in his murder my crimes are consummated; the miserable series of my being is wound to its close...Oh, Frankenstein, generous and self-devoted being! What does it avail that I now ask thee to pardon me? (14)

Walton, who has surprised the Monster in Frankenstein's death cabin, describes him as "gigantic in stature, yet uncouth and distorted in proportions." Walton is so overcome by the loathsomeness that he shuts his eyes, endeavoring to collect his thoughts and determine his obligations. Hate may indeed be as strong a reason for living as love. Now that Frankenstein is dead, it is with real determination that the Monster plots his own end. After indicating to Walton his plans, he goes on to contemplate an almost mystical union with Frankenstein in death. It is here most evident that his maker is fully this Monster's god.

Though Mary Shelley lacked the grand rhetorical style, she did give her Monster the proper words to prepare for a Stoic suicide. With his immortal longings upon him, he looks peacefully to the moment when he will ascend his funeral pyre and welcome the agony of the flames, after which his spirit will finally "sleep in peace."

Readers sometimes speculate why Mary, who had previously shown no hesitancy to describe the death agonies of her characters, left a slight ambiguity in the death of the Monster. There is no indication that she ever contemplated a sequel, though Leonard Wolf, for one, has postulated a subconscious attachment that made it impossible for her to kill off the Monster in cold blood as she had done other characters. While most readers and even literary historians will take the Monster at his word, assuming that he indeed ended his miserable life as promised, the reader never really sees him die or hears any report that he has done so. Thus, the way is paved for the innumerable "returns," "sons," and "brides" of Frankenstein. Mary herself resisted any temptation she may have had, despite the success of her story, to further exploit her unhappy creature. The cinema, though it has usually changed the circumstances of the conclusion of the tale, has shown no such reticence.

Resonances of Frankenstein

The readings and experiences of Mary Shelley's nineteen years flowed into her narrative, which David Ketterer has aptly described as a "loose and baggy monster," put together from classical myths (particularly the contradictory ones the ancients related about Prometheus); Christian narratives, chiefly as interpreted by Milton; Gothic romances, with hints of unspeakable depravity and horror, suggestions of *doppelgangers* and unallowed science; and popular novels, with their domestic misfortunes, obstacles to courtship, and precarious marriages. Other influences, blended oddly with the Godwinian and Wollstonecraftian doctrines, included Erasmus Darwin, in whose name scientific marvels were conjured; John Locke, whose theories of education, when applied to the Monster, received a test even that philosopher could not have envisioned; and, of course, Jean-Jacques Rousseau, whose notion of the Natural Man turned awry led to the Monster's characterization.

Any wide reader of the literature of Mary's period would also discern echoes of "Monk" Lewis's lurid romances, of Coleridge's poems "Christabel" and, more especially, "The Rhyme of the Ancient Mariner," and of the romances of the American Gothic novelist William Godwin so much admired, Charles Brockden Brown.

Despite the amazement of Mary's first readers at her originality and the fact that we still marvel at her fecund imagination, the idea of an artificial man goes back to ancient occult theories and classical myths. By Mary's own time, there were serious speculations in scientific research about the possibility that the "divine spark" of life might be discovered to be electrical or quasi-electrical and capable of transmission through electrical current, Galvinism, or some related process. Scientists whose names the layman liked to associate with such speculation included, in addition to Darwin, Sir Humphrey Davy, Luigi Galvani, and Count Alessandra Volta.

But Mary's mind was more in tune with classical myth than with modern science. In Switzerland she would no doubt have viewed the automatons then in vogue, those clever animated dolls fashioned by that nation of watchmakers. Some danced, while others played musical instruments or games like chess. They would have reminded her again of the myth of Pygmalion, the legendary king of Cyprus who fell in love with a female statue he had made. Through the powers of the goddess Aphrodite, his prayers were answered and life entered his statue. Since Pygmalion gave all credit to the goddess and did not pridefully offend, he was allowed to live happily with his female creature.

There is no evidence that Mary Shelley ever heard the Golem legends of the East European Jews. They were, however, greatly influence the early Frankenstein films, and in this way integrate themselves into the expanding body of popular lore surrounding Mary's Monster. According to Jewish legend, the Golem was an artificial man made of clay and brought to life by the head rabbi of Prague through cabbalistic ritual and the use of the Holy Name. Though God-ordained, lifebestowing powers were used, they were wrongfully employed, with dire results. The Golem, a creature of enormous strength and lofty stature, had been originally designed to protect the Jewish community at holiday time from their rampaging Gentile oppressors. But the rabbi had been unable to control his creature, which was soon running amok in the streets of Prague. The Golem had to be stilled by withdrawing the Holy Name in another cabbalistic ceremony.

Radu Florescu, in his vast, entertaining collection of lore entitled *In Search of Frankenstein*, decided to investigate the name "Frankenstein." It was not hard to discover that it belonged to an illustrious German family, probably totally unknown to Mary. The family still exists, with no more skeletons in their closets than any other great European house. The thirteenth-century ancestral castle of the Barons Frankenstein may still be seen in the Rhine Valley and may or may not have been visited by the Shelleys. (15)

Florescu suggests several reasons why Mary may have chosen the name. "Frankheim" and "Falkenstein" were characters in tales written by "Monk" Lewis. Benjamin Franklin, the American wizard who experimented with electricity, could have provided another association. Though the Frankenstein family of Mary's novel are Swiss, and therefore have no fancy aristocratic titles, the name held a sinister German fascination for English-speaking audiences, steeped in the Gothic romance. Later on, two world wars with Germany would enhance the negatively dramatic associations for British and American people. During World War II, in fact, the Allies even used Frankenstein adaptations as part of their wartime propaganda, distributing them to men in uniform. It is significant that while the various film adaptations have changed practically everything else in the original tale, the name Frankenstein has never been relinquished. (16)

Responses to Frankenstein

It was hard at first to find a publisher for the book, which is known to have been rejected by at least three houses. For instance, the reader to whom Byron's publisher gave it found the narrative too radical in tone. Shelley finally managed to place the manuscript with a house that was known to traffic in the more sensational romances, especially those dealing with the occult and necromancy.

Though it bore a dedication to William Godwin, the book was published anonymously. Many readers believed it to be Shelley's own work, considering its flamboyant material and dedication. Few guessed Frankenstein to be the work of a woman.

According to the practice of the time, the text was issued in three separate small volumes. They sold rapidly. Despite this immediate popular success, serious reviews at first were generally negative. William Gifford of the influential Quarterly Review found the book too socially and politically shocking for him to recommend to his readers; he discovered no useful lessons to be learned in the way of "conduct, manners, or morality." (17)

The Edinburgh Magazine was more favorable, speaking of the narrative's "power of fascination" and "mastery in harsh and savage delineations of passion." (18) Though intrigued, the reviewer still had his reservations, wondering how such a book might have come to be written and bewildered by the possible motivations of the author.

Shelley sent a copy to Sir Walter Scott, the grand old man

of historical romance who reviewed it with praise, calling it "a extraordinary tale...expressed in plain and forcible English whose author exhibited "uncommon powers of poetic imagination Scott found the narrative "wild in incident" and admitted it ha shaken even his firm nerves a bit. He especially liked th descriptions of landscapes, perhaps sensing the inspiration c the wild regions of Scotland. He, like others, believed Shelle to be the author and generously acknowledged that he preferre *Frankenstein* to his own romances.

Only on one point did Scott have reservations. He felt tha both the self-education of the Monster and the extent of h unimpeded destructiveness strained credibility. (19)

Almost as interesting as *Frankenstein* itself has been th literature that has subsequently grown up around the provocativ novel. Every critical persuasion, it would seem, has provided new interpretation, often set forth with near-religious enthus iasm. Academic essayists have sometimes approached Mary's narra tive, condescension mingled with awe, confident that at last the can produce the definitive interpretation. Yet the book sti refuses to yield its full and final secrets.

A few of the most influential, or unusual, readings of th work are worth mentioning. Harold Bloom's "Afterword" to th Signet Classics edition calls attention to that which should hav been obvious to all but really has not been, the book's echo c classical myth. Mary did not lightly designate Frankenstein "th modern Prometheus." In early Christianity, the Promethean figu from pagan mythology was given antithetical symbolic and typolo gical status. Prometheus was viewed as a type both of Lucife and of Christ, possessing a dual nature. While he was the bene factor of man, with his gift of fire, he was also a rebel again the gods, from whom he stole that fire. Victor Frankenstei wanted to give the secret of life to man so that the dead coul be reanimated, yet in doing so he usurped the prerogatives c God.

Perhaps the most influential statement of the importance c *Frankenstein* to science fiction has come from Brian W. Aldis who, in his *Billion Year Spree: The True History of Scienc Fiction*, calls Mary the founder of the entire genre. The fir and most significant chapter of the Aldiss book is appropriatel entitled "The Origin of the Species: Mary Shelley." Writing n only as a scholar, but as a successful novelist in the genr Aldiss knows the expectations of the science-fiction audienc He acknowledges that this relatively new mode of fictional explo ration, as much evolutionary as technological, is not yet totall free of the Gothic *milieu* in which it was born on the banks c Lake Geneva. Science fiction hastens to provide a rationalist explanation of its marvels, not totally unlike the Gothic romanc which often explained away the seemingly supernatural at the enc There are other neat parallels, such as the love of exotic adven ture (Mars being substituted for Spain) and amorous entanglemen with aliens, whether Venutians or Italians.

In part it may be literary nationalism that leads Aldiss, a

Englishman, to credit his homeland with the birth of the genre most of the world regards as characteristically American, but as a skilled practitioner as well as a theorist of science fiction, he speaks with an authority that cannot be ignored.

Few people better understand popular taste than Stephen King, the high-energy, contemporary best-selling horror author. In his informative, though ramblingly impressionistic *Danse Macabre*, he treats Mary Shelley with respectful attention, marveling that *Frankenstein* has inspired more films than any other literary work, including the Bible, and has become a part of the "American myth pool." King is also amused by the discrepancy between the inarticulate monster of the films and "Shelley's creature" who "speaks with the rotund, balanced phrases of a peer of the House of Lords or William F. Buckley disputing politely with Dick Cavett on a TV talk show." King aptly notes that Mary preferred the realm of ideas and was at her best when Victor Frankenstein and his creature argued the pros and cons of that controversial request for a mate "like Harvard debaters." His best observation—in fact it is a profound one—is that the narrative falls short by its lack of unity of intent and, thereby, fails to achieve the high tragic tone to which its author aspired. This fault is the result of Mary's uncertainty as to just where to locate the fatal flaw: is it Victor's *hubris* in seizing a power rightfully belonging only to God, or is it his unwillingness to take responsibility for the creature he had made? (20)

Paul A. Carter, in *The Creation of Tomorrow: Fifty Years of Magazine Science Fiction*, has stressed, possibly overstressed, Mary's "home-brewed concoction" as the precursor of Karel Capek's *R.U.R.* and of countless magazine robots which are mass produced and no longer organic in structure. It is a long though direct path, he feels, from *Frankenstein* to Ray Bradbury's benign baby-sitting grandmother robot or his robotic house, which still performs its functions after its human inhabitants have been destroyed in thermonuclear war. Science-fiction magazine fiction, as Carter amply documents and as every reader already knows, is filled with these humanoid creatures he calls Frankenstein's descendants.

Baird Searles, Martin Last, Beth Meacham, and Michael Franklin, in their reference book, *A Reader's Guide to Science Fiction*, see *Frankenstein* basically as a cautionary tale. The Enlightenment had proclaimed the power of human reason to sweep away superstition, while the Industrial Revolution had promised universal prosperity through the amazing efficiency of production. But Mary intuitively understood that science and industrial progress alone present serious dangers. Thus *Frankenstein*, that "mutant child of the Gothic novel," is both the first major science-fiction novel and yet an anti-progress novel which expresses strong fear of science. The scientist thus becomes a major villain of popular culture, a possible enemy of the human race.

Robert Scholes and Eric S. Rabkin in *Science Fiction: History, Science, Vision* observe how Frankenstein as a young science student proceeds with a twofold motivation: he is a pure scientist obsessed with acquiring knowledge for its own sake, yet he also desires that the fruits of his research improve the human stock. His tale becomes an encounter between the "two cultures." Not only is he less capable as a philosopher and a human being than he is as a scientist, but he clearly becomes the Faustian seeker who rushes to his damnation. The movies, less troubled by ambivalences and ambiguities than was Mary, were to reiterate, in many shadowy caverns and cavernous laboratories, the pronouncement so clearly yet more complexly implied in the novel that "there are some things it is not meant for men to know."

Robert M. Philmus, in his fine, if somewhat dated book, *Into the Unknown: The Evolution of Science Fiction from Francis Godwin to H.G. Wells*, views *Frankenstein* as the *reductio ad absurdum* of the ethical theory enunciated by Godwin, to whom Mary so lovingly dedicated her book. In rejecting traditional religious sanctions, Godwin had attempted to establish morality on the basis of human psychology, grounding his ethic on the fact that man is essentially a social being and declaring: "No being can be either virtuous, or vicious, who has no opportunity of influencing the happiness of others." The Monster follows Godwin's principle with a Satanic logic; he can only establish relationship with others by setting his hand against them, bringing them misery and death.

All too often the stylistic features of *Frankenstein* have been casually dismissed, so strong has been the tendency to view the work as a powerful myth badly imparted. Patrick Parrinder in *Science Fiction: Its Criticism and Teaching* observes that Mary cleverly uses the forms of the journal and epistle to achieve verisimilitude, tricks learned from the popular romances of her period. Her use of these forms is perhaps even more effective than her attempt to achieve credibility through pseudo-scientific allusions. The voice which speaks in her book is not that of the remote narrator of a Germanic or American tall tale but of the "eye witness" observer that readers had found so convincing in *Gulliver's Travels* and the writings of DeFoe. Although today *Frankenstein* does not appear to be the model of stylistic restraint that Sir Walter Scott, for example, found it, it does attempt to make itself convincing through its homey forms of narrative, much as Poe, Wells, and, later, Kafka, were painstakingly to strive for believability by recounting extravagant incidents with the deadpan use of the prosaic styles of the travelogue, the ship's log, the newspaper article, the scientific report, and the bureaucratic memo.

Few writings on *Frankenstein* in the last few years have received more attention that the late Ellen Moers' essay "Female Gothic," which first appeared as a single article and was later incorporated into *Literary Women*, her provocative book on female writers. (21) Moers finds significance in the fact that *Frankenstein* is the work of a young wife and mother in a time when most female authors in England and America were spinsters or childless matrons. Whatever else it may be, Moers sees the story primarily as "a birth myth" and a somewhat dark one at that. Though Mary deeply loved her children, her early experience in motherhood was fraught with anxiety. She was unmarried and pregnant at the age of sixteen. For the next five years, she was almost constantly pregnant, sometimes uncomfortably so, though by now she had become a properly wedded wife. Most of her children perished soon after birth, and shortly before Shelley's own death, it will be remembered, she suffered a painful miscarriage. While all these facts would not bear directly on the first edition of the novel, they would certainly have applied by the time Mary, as a widow, revised her work. Yet even when the first lines of *Frankenstein* were penned, Mary would have been recalling that her own mother had died, horribly and unexpectedly, at the time of her own birth. Moers believes that in *Frankenstein* Mary expressed subconscious revulsion against newborn life, pouring into her dramatic narrative all the guilt, dread, fear, and trauma she associated with childbirth. In considering Moers' thesis, it is well to remember that *Frankenstein* is definitely that tale of absent mothers and life that is created without female assistance. If Moers is correct, young Frankenstein's rooms, described as a "workshop of filthy creation," are a profound image expressing Mary's own fear of sexuality and its sometimes bitter consequences.

Kate Ellis provides another highly-convincing feminist reading of the book in "Monsters in the Garden: Mary Shelley and the Bourgeois Family." Ellis feels that the writings of Wollstonecraft were perhaps the dominant influence on Mary's thought. When Wollstonecraft viewed the institution of marriage as it existed during her time, she saw domestic affection undermined by exaggerated sex role differentiation. In *Frankenstein* some of Wollstonecraft's ideas are placed into action in the rather idealized portrait of the DeLacey family in which, though again there is no matriarchal figure present, males and females live and study together with minimal role distinctions. They are truly companions and intellectual peers. When Safie fled Turkish harem life, it was not to isolate herself in a traditional Swiss domestic setting.

Lee Sterrenburg, in "Mary Shelley's Monster: Politics and Psyche in *Frankenstein*" sees Mary rejecting rather than affirming parental doctrines. Sterrenburg believes Mary is much more courageously original than generally believed. The utopian and radical heritage of Godwin proves inadequate to her. Godwin's vision of a new day when restraining institutions will be dissolved and oppression will, therefore, come to an end is apparently not shared by his daughter. Though institutions, particularly the courts, do not function too effectively or justly in her novel, there is no indication that suitable replacements are on the way, and the family is still the social unit in which all characters ardently long for participation.

Godwin's writings at least suggested the possibility that humans might reasonably aspire to immortality once the pressures of over-population were brought under control and scientific progress was well advanced. There is little of that grandiose optimism in his daughter's narrative. Science rather than kindly prolonging human life introduces more problems than it solves, and individual cruelty more than the indifference of social institutions seems to be the root of evil.

Peter Dale Scott in "Vital Artifice: Mary, Percy, and the Psychopolitical Integrity of *Frankenstein*" finds the book less influenced, either positively or negatively, by Mary's parents than by that other "insensitive but idealistic Utopian, her father's disciple, Percy Bysshe Shelley." Scott feels that both the creature and Victor Frankenstein resemble Shelley in their total self-absorption. So great is their sense of grievance that they are unable to reach beyond it to practice any of the great Stoic or Christian virtues. Not only is selfishness the fatal flaw; the social *milieu* of the Frankenstein world is overly-masculinized. Scott feels that Mary was able to transform her personal responses to a dominating father, an absent mother, and an imbalanced husband into a compassionate but not uncritical fictional study of a male-dominated society. "One might even say," adds Scott, "that the novel describes Victor's fall as Androgyny Lost, and that it at least offers the prospect of an Androgyny Regained." (22)

Connoisseurs of the Universal Studios classic films have frequently pointed to *Abbott and Costello Meet Frankenstein* as the ultimate demeaning of their noble monster. They have looked with disdain on the tag-end films where the old monsters no longer terrify but are made the butt of crude gags. Philip Stevick, in an unusual if not always convincing essay, "*Frankenstein* and Comedy" feels that humor legitimately arises from the book. Most readers have, of course, found *Frankenstein* utterly serious in both content and execution, lacking even comic relief. Stevick, however, feels there is a grotesque joke implied in the presentation of Victor as one of the world's great scientists, the equal of a Darwin or an Einstein. "Frankenstein," says Stevick, "is a failure, not in the grand and tragic manner but in a manner closer to low comedy, bumbling, inattentive, inept, and ineffectual." (23)

After admitting that Mary's novel is remarkably static—with excessive amounts of talk, many flat passages, and overlong explanations—Stevick observes that Frankenstein himself does get about: he walks, rides, is conveyed in a chaise and in a cabriolet. Even more frequently, he seems to be riding in boats. The Monster moves forward still more speedily, on his own steam, totally unlike the slow, leaden-footed creature of the films. Much territory is covered by both Frankenstein and the Monster. With this farcical pace at which the characters move, gaucheries abound. Many readers with reason have regarded the book as glorious camp. For example, Stevick notes the scene in which the miserable, perishing Frankenstein is pulled from the icy sea by Walton. His first words to his benefactor are: "Before I come aboard your vessel...will you please have the kindness to inform me whither you are bound?"

NOTES

1. Harold Bloom, ed., *Frankenstein; or The Modern Prometheus* (New York: The New American Library, 1965), viii.

2. Ibid., ix.

3. Ibid., xii.

4. Ibid., x.

5. Ibid., xi.

6. Leonard Wolf, ed., *The Annotated Frankenstein* (New York: Clarkson N. Potter, 1977), p. 77.

7. Ibid., p. 171.

8. Ibid., p. 213.

9. Ibid., p. 186.

10. Ibid., p. 140.

11. Ibid., p. 213.

12. Ibid., p. 72.

13. Ibid., p. 324.

14. Ibid., p. 320.

15. Radu Florescu, *In Search of Frankenstein* (Boston: New York Graphic Society, 1975), pp. 34-35.

16. Today Frankenstein families consider the novel and the movies it spawned an embarrassment. Understandably, they tire of the endless jokes they must endure. The present writer once had a handsome Ms. Frankenstein enrolled in a course. Upon the first roll call the rest of the class roared with laughter at mention of the name. Ms. Frankenstein's imperious, scathing glares, however, quickly silenced the jokesters.

17. Cited by William A. Walling, *Mary Shelley* (Boston: Twayne Publishers, 1972), p. 33.

18. *Edinburgh Magazine* (March 1818), cited by Walling, p. 34.

19. *Blackwood's Edinburgh Magazine* (March 1818), cited in Wal-

ling, p. 34.

20. Stephen King, *Danse Macabre* (New York: Berkley Books, 1983), p. 53.

21. Essays by Moers, *et al.* have been collected in *The Endurance of Frankenstein; Essays on Mary Shelley's Novel*, ed. by George Levine and U.C. Knoepflmacher (Berkeley: University of California Press, 1974).

22. Ibid., p. 189.

23. Ibid., p. 225.

V
"FEARSOME PROGENY"

Radu Florescu has accurately observed that a "Frankenstein explosion" has taken place in recent decades, often having little to do with established Shelley scholarship. While academicians have contributed their articles to the *Shelley-Keats Journal* and occasionally have written more popular pieces for the mass circulation and feminist magazines, proving various serious points and advancing looser theses, fans and enthusiasts, such as Forrest Ackerman and Donald Glut, have compiled and catalogued Frankensteiniana. Artists have imaginatively illustrated new editions of the book, expanding its range rather than merely depicting it. Original made-for-television productions have appeared with some regularity. Fictional books, by people like Kerek Marlowe, Brian Aldiss, and Anne Edwards, have further advanced the Frankenstein mythos.

Translations of *Frankenstein* have appeared in all major languages and in the more exotic tongues of Czech, Flemish, Urdu, and Malaysian, to mention a few. There is even a Rumanian edition of *Frankenstein*, though no text of *Dracula* is yet available in that language, despite the Rumanian monster tourist trade. Numerous recordings have featured Boris Karloff and other actors reading portions of the text. Film spinoffs have included Blacksploitation films, such as *Blackenstein*, a number of straight parodies, as well as independent underground, pornographic, and transvestite camp productions.

Of course, it is through the movies that *Frankenstein* has become a part of the popular culture and a myth of Western society. The films owe the stage a debt: there was already an impressive stage history for the narrative before Karloff's monster ever opened his eyes. Between 1823, the date of the second edition of the novel, and the present time, well over fifty-eight dramatizations of the story, many of them highly effective, have been performed in the English-speaking world.

Writers, directors, makeup artists, and many others work quietly behind the scenes, and it is their skill which often assures the success of stage and cinema productions. Yet it is the skilled actor that the audience remembers and long afterward still credits with a fine evening of entertainment. The dramatic success of the Frankenstein narrative cannot readily be understood unless proper attention is given to T.P. Cooke, who, beginning in 1823, definitively interpreted the Monster on stage, and Boris Karloff, whose name can never be separated from the Monster's film image. Because of the necessary limitations of his medium, Cooke never became world famous, as Karloff was to become after his films of the 1930's were seen in every hamlet and village. Nevertheless, Cooke was the precursor who horrified and titillated audiences through many performances, giving the stamp of his personality and artistry to the role. From all accounts, Cooke's appearance on the stage was impressively fearsome, his heavy stage makeup giving his face a greenish-yellow glow around dull, watery eyes. His terrible grimace and straight black lips were objects of much discussion. Cooke's acting was also described by his contemporaries as inventive and powerful. Just as Karloff was later to reveal himself a master of cinema style, Cooke knew how to convey horror on the stage, projecting his mood of terror and decadence even while he was able to stir in the audience some sympathy for the Monster's plight.

Cooke's awakening scene, done in pantomime, was labeled brilliant by the critics of his time, who marveled at his ability to suggest the beginning awareness of sense impressions and emotions. Cooke's art was compared in its beauty and terror to the painting of Henry Fuseli, that old inamorato of Wollstonecraft. Though the play had a long run, Cooke eventually tired of his role and finally managed to escape typecasting by returning to the nautical parts in which he had earlier distinguished himself.

The finest asset of the first two Universal Studios *Frankenstein* films, apart from their brilliant director, James Whale, was, of course, Boris Karloff. Other actors who have had the similar experience of becoming associated with one startling and eccentric role have sometimes complained that Hollywood's tendency to typecast has stifled or even ruined promising careers. But Karloff, who was never heard to voice this frustration, seems to have developed a special affection for the Monster, who lifted him from his status as a featured player and transformed him into a world-famous actor.

Boris Karloff was, outside the movie theatre, a cultivated, witty, rather shy Englishman who was an authority on children's literature. He possessed a nobly sculptured face and a deep, resonant voice, attributes little used in his most famous role. Credit for perceiving Karloff's scare potential goes to director James Whale who spotted him on the Universal lot at work on a minor gangster picture. The Hungarian actor Bela Lugosi had already turned down the part of the Frankenstein Monster. After exuding sexuality as Dracula, Lugosi had established himself as a horror star who was also a matinee idol rivaling Clark Gable in popularity. Understandably, he did not wish his fans to see him as a deformed monster.

Filmmakers have generally been eager to associate their works with classics of literature as well as best-selling novels, despite their tendency to play fast and loose with their literary materials, adapting them not only to the requirements of the film medium but even the expectations of a popular audience, or what those expectations are felt to be. Whale's film quite appropriately bears a stronger relationship to the time in which it was made, reflecting the economic turmoil of the early 1930's, than to the special social, artistic, and even scientific world of the Shelleys. It is also an escape entertainment, too ambivalent in working out its themes to provoke the deep thought Mary Shelley sought to stir. Yet the stark visual beauty of the film and its cathartic acts of violence have never lost their power.

Whale was not only a skilled maker of popular films; he was a highly competent artist who appropriately used the techniques which had been developed by the pioneers of the cinema, such as Griffith, Eisenstein, and Murnau. In his original *Frankenstein* of 1932, he relied most on the German traditions of the grotesque and the visual conventions of German Expressionism. His strong visual allusions to the German film *The Golem* are especially evident.

Whale's second Frankenstein film, with Karloff again in the role of the Monster, has been preferred by many students of the cinema to his original. *Bride of Frankenstein* is almost Wagnerian in musical score, yet is tinged with self-parody. Whale directed his experienced stage actors as if they were performing Shakespeare. Elsa Lancaster's brief appearance as a dazzling Monsteress, intended bride of the Monster, has also been justly praised. The 1935 sequel was further notable in that it opened with a prologue in which Lancaster also played an elegant, drawing-room Mary Shelley, introducing the narrative to Percy Bysshe and Lord Byron, and consequently to the public.

While Whale's first two Frankenstein films are widely regarded as the most distinguished of the genre, perhaps the only Frankenstein films to qualify as genuine works of art, they were, as every movie fan knows, only the beginning. In the 1950's Hammer Studios in England remade the Universal Studios horror classics in full color, using visual tricks that had evolved in the intervening years of cinema experimentation. Though the terrors could now be made more vividly visual, most of the poetry of the older films eluded the new filmmakers. Almost all cinema enthusiasts have preferred Whale's interplay of light and shadow to the vivid gore provided by Technicolor.

Many explanations continue to be suggested for the persistence of the Frankenstein films, the re-releases, and the endless remakes and adaptations. The films have often been good entertainment, replete with visual surprises and rapidly-paced scenarios. They have explored tensions, fears, desires, threats of isolation and rejection, forbidden titillations, and possibly even hidden death wishes. It has been suggested that more viewers identify with the Monster, in his aloneness and hideousness, than with Frankenstein, in his prideful agony. This may be the reason Karloff's image is conjured by the imagination every time the name "Frankenstein" is mentioned, while, after some years have passed, it is hard to visualize the face of Colin Clive or any other actor who played Victor Frankenstein himself.

Like a few other works of modern literature which have established a mythos—the writings of H.P. Lovecraft come to mind—*Frankenstein* has provided the inspiration and starting point for the work of more writers. Anne Edwards' *Haunted Summer* is a historical-biographical novel, somewhat pedestrian but well researched, which purports to tell how *Frankenstein* came to be written. Edwards sees Mary Shelley's novel as not only an imitation of the German Gothic romance but, more significantly, as the expression of the troubled psyches of the entire Shelley circle at the time it was composed. Lord Byron and Polidori feature prominently in Edwards' romance, along with Mary herself and Percy Bysshe.

Frankenstein Unbound is a genuine science-fiction romance by Brian W. Aldiss, the writer who has given Mary such generous credit for founding the genre he successfully contributes to. Aldiss leaves the reader with the feeling that he is a bit in love with Mary, impressed by her beauty and vulnerability, as well as her original imagination. In his own narrative, a time-traveler from the twenty-first century succeeds in having an affair with Mary during a time slip which throws him back to early nineteenth-century Geneva. There the traveler discovers that Dr. Frankenstein and his nameless Monster are as real as the Shelleys themselves.

Several interesting philosophical questions are suggested by the visit of this hero from 2020 A.D., from a world where politicians are playing war games with another Frankenstein-like monster that threatens total human annihilation. The timetripping hero who discovers himself caught up in a nineteenth-century Gothic romance finds the Frankenstein world to be no more terrifying than the precarious dystopia from which he has come.

A third work of particular interest generated by Mary's tale is a teleplay by Christopher Isherwood and Don Bachardy. When it was first shown on American television, its advertising somewhat falsely intimated that it faithfully copied the "classic novel by Mary W. Shelley," and it was misnamed *Frankenstein: The True Story*.

Though unfaithful to Mary's original conception, the Isherwood-Bachardy drama is a fine tale in its own right, with some good climactic moments for television and a meaningful exploration of some serious themes, akin to those Mary herself introduced. The authors clearly set out to "improve" the original rather than merely dramatize it appropriately for the "tube." They added several sets which are particularly effective. The education of the Monster, an adult first experiencing life, is more convincingly and meaningfully imagined than in Mary's novel. The monsteress is brought to life as a lady of surpassing beauty and ability to dazzle human society.

There are also some memorable symbolic uses of the Bible. For example, in one scene the Monster hears a peasant woman reading the Gospels and, in a later scene, when asked his name, he quotes: "My name is Legion." At another point, Elizabeth, Frankenstein's fiancée as usual, heavyhandedly kills an artificially revivified butterfly she sees in Frankenstein's laboratory by swatting it with a Bible.

As stage, cinema, and television have repeatedly demonstrated, *Frankenstein* offers innumerable possibilities for visual art: its prose is filled with imaginative images, and there are splendid dramatic panoramas. It is not hard to understand why several distinguished illustrators have been called to interpret "this flawed but powerful novel." (1)

In the original 1818 edition of *Frankenstein*, there were no illustrations, but the revised edition of 1831 had a frontispiece and a title page decoration, the work of Chevalier, a popular illustrator of the time. His drawings bore no particular relevance to the narrative and could have served equally well for *Hamlet*, *The Sorrows of Young Werther*, or innumerable other gloomy works of love and death.

Only in the twentieth century, when more improved procedures for reproducing art works were developed, did illustrators of prominence contribute noteworthy work to *Frankenstein* editions.

Nino Carbe made some woodcuts for a 1932 Illustrated Editions publication. Sparce and dignified, they convey effectively the agony and loneliness of the novel's principal characters. Because they are tasteful and restrained, even understated, they have not become dated.

In 1934 two important illustrated editions appeared. Lynd Ward, especially acclaimed for his work in children's books, contributed to the Harison Smith-Robert Haas editions. Ward made strongly outlined woodblock prints which captured the story's stark, muscular power and suggested something of its mythical dimension. Leonard Wolf commends the "megalithic quality" of Ward's work.

Everett Henry's pastels for another edition of the same year are quite different but equally valid and interesting. Henry's work graced the Limited Editions Club printing; volumes in this series were noted for their unusual illustrations. While Henry's medium was possibly less appropriate than the woodblock for conveying the Promethean themes of the narrative, his work had charm and even touches of humor. The Monster was wisely left as little more than a shadowy, implied presence.

Foreign editions have sometimes been illustrated with special artistry. In 1968, Christian Broutin made some pen and ink drawings for the French *Cercle du Bibliophile* edition. Broutin's work is adult, grimly horrifying, and suggests the *fleur de mal* decadence of a Baudelaire. More than any other illustrator he understood the dark sensuality Mary's novel implied. Claude Selva's 1969 drawings for the Swiss *Editions d'Erable* have also been described as darkly intimate and highly psychological.

In 1976 Robert Andrew Parker provided some watercolors for the Clarkson N. Potter coffee table volume, *The Illustrated Frankenstein*. Parker's work has been widely praised, for its mock simplicity and its image of the Monster as a gigantic, even slightly comic presence against the Swiss mountain glaciers. Marcia Huyette's full-page black and white illustrations which so enhance Leonard Wolf's *The Annotated Frankenstein* deserve attention for their skillful oommunication of the horror of the narrative, its mythic power, and its major themes.

One of the most appealing recent versions is the Dodd Mead *Mary Wollstonecraft Shelley's Frankenstein*, 1983, with illustrations by Berni Wrightson, who is famous for his work in comic books. Wrightson maintains the right visual balance between the nineteenth-century mystery or domestic novel and the Gothic romance. Exotic locales—distant snowy mountains, frigid glaciers, and Arctic ice fields, in which the frozen masts of ships are entangled—are all well depicted. The mood of loneliness which so dominates the book is consistently conveyed, frequently by drawings which isolate very small human figures against immense natural settings or architectural structures. Frankenstein himself is a sensitive, disheveled young man, often pictured as a solitary figure against those overpowering natural and manmade backdrops. Closeup portraits of the Monster reveal a face somewhat poignantly Karloffian, as is perhaps inevitable from this time forward. Yet in his encounters with others, the Monster is drawn huge and horrible; here the full power of the former comic book artist is evident.

Wrightson is to be commended for his faithful rendering of Mary's work, at the same time that his art expands the emotional response of the reader. A dark, perverse sensuality pervades the wedding night murder scene, though there is no open indelicacy. Wrightson does not neglect the Swiss pastoral scenes and moods, understanding well the quaint domestic features of the narrative. A lone woman weeps beside a tomb in a wintery cemetery, reminding the collector of old books of early illustrations of another pastoral horror story, *Uncle Tom's Cabin*.

Frankenstein's "laboratory of filthy creation" is drawn precisely and literally, as the phrase describes it. Victor's professor has a library filled with stacks of filthy, rotting books, outward images and symbols of a decadent spiritual state. Even the Rhine, from Strasbourg to Rotterdam, becomes gloomy and spirit-haunted in Wrightson's sketches. One could easily imagine it populated by Wagnerian monsters.

These illustrations do not neglect the pathos of the Creature either. In the scene where he dances around a fire he has lit to destroy a rural cabin, the primitive quality of an authentic religious rite of antiquity is conveyed. The Monster's despair is evident in several drawings which concentrate on his longings and misfortunes, his deformity, and his rejection by humankind. The Monster and Frankenstein confront each other dramatically on the icy wastes, and Wrightson cleverly allows the creature to tower far above his maker, greater not only in stature but in mind and even spirit.

NOTES

1. Much useful information on *Frankenstein* illustrations may be found in Leonard Wolf's *The Annotated Frankenstein* (New York: Clarkson N. Potter, 1977), pp. 347-349.

VI
THE LAST MAN:
APOCALYPSE AND FALSE PROPHECY

Though no other writing of Mary Shelley's substantial literary career approaches *Frankenstein* in influence, mythic power, or popularity, her novel *The Last Man*, published in 1826, is of considerable interest to the science-fiction audience and is perhaps more topical today than at the time it was written. Though it has always received substantially less attention than the earlier novel, *The Last Man* is almost equally germinal in science-fiction ideas. It is usually discussed as "apocalyptic fiction" and placed within that familiar category, yet it is, among other things, also Mary's expression of the Romantic myth of the solitary man. Again she inverts a romantic ideal; her vision of the man alone stresses his grim solitude rather than his admirable self-sufficiency.

The Last Man can be meaningfully compared with other well-known writings without suggesting that it directly influenced every subsequent work of similar plot. For example, it is unlikely to have had any bearing at all on Albert Camus' twentieth-century parable *La Peste*, which is more about man's struggle against his destructiveness than his elimination from the planet. Camus' novel does resemble Mary's work in mood, atmosphere, and even in the pace of its plot development. However, Mary's work has more direct connection with Nevil Shute's *On the Beach*, in which a group of Australians, who seem to be the last survivors of thermonuclear war, await their own end through fallout poison. Shute's writing speaks more immediately to our contemporary fears than does Mary's, and his explanation of the end of the human race is today the more plausible. We no longer very much fear the extinction of our kind through disease—though occasionally a science-fiction writer can still cause shivers by importing a virus from outer space for which we have no immunities. Yet while we have considerable faith in modern medical science to cure disease, we truly lack confidence in our ability to control atomic energy. Stories predicated on our end through modern warfare thus are particularly convincing and terrifying.

Mary herself was certainly influenced by the writings of Daniel DeFoe. She makes direct reference in her own novel to DeFoe's *The Journal of the Plague Year*, and we know from her journal entries that she had recently read *Robinson Crusoe* and was probably as gripped by its narrative of a lone survivor as most readers past or present have been.

The Last Man opens in a setting which appears to be a fulfillment of all William Godwin's optimistic prophesying of the future. In the last decade of the twenty-first century, people are living extremely well. They travel in air balloons and are quickly transported in boats from one place to another through convenient canals. Gifted engineers are also busy constructing fine bridges. Programs that promise to totally abolish poverty are well under way, and disease seems under control. Technology has enabled food to be produced on a large scale, efficiently and inexpensively. For the first time in history, it appears possible to adequately provide the necessities of life for the earth's entire population. Nobody is more joyful than Adrian, the son of England's last king, who foresees a universal era of peace, freedom, abundance, and health. In this age of the common man, the monarchy has been peacefully abolished, and Adrian, happy to be the peer of everyone else, proclaims that very soon "Earth will become a Paradise." He observes that for the first time in history energies are being directed toward liberation and preservation rather than the mutilation and destruction of the species.

The reader quickly notes that Mary's powers of futuristic prophecy are severely limited. She foresees a technology that brings abundant food production, though she is vague on the details. She understands that there will be facilitated transportation, though here as well she has no grasp of the methods by which this will indeed come about. She may be naive in believing that the humanistic aspirations of the Enlightenment can be realized, that kings will give up their thrones without struggle and that the selfishness of social classes will vanish. None of the real marvels and terrors of the future, as the people of today are actually experiencing it, are anticipated by her. There are no airplanes in her novel, no computers, no imaginative sources of energy, or organ transplants. No new forms of communication, art, or entertainment have been invented. Neither are there atomic bombs, criminal enclaves, acts of international terrorism, widescale pollutions, nor shortages of energy.

Though Mary may be naive about human unselfishness, she is far from being an optimist. Nature itself brings this Utopian world swiftly to a halt. A plague originating mysteriously in the East enters Europe, and in less than a decade, by the end of the novel, only one human remains alive. He is Lionel Verney, identified by some knowledgeable readers as a male alter ego for Mary herself, though others have seen him as yet another fictional portrait of Shelley. Verney's friend, Lord Raymond, seems remarkably like Lord Byron, who had died a hero's death in the cause of Greek independence just about the time Mary was writing *The Last Man.*

Mary's narrative describes the endtime with some vividness. Not much dignity and nobility of human conduct are evident in the crisis. The old raw energies of human nature, the tooth-and-claw struggles for survival, which had been temporarily subdued, manifest themselves again. Perhaps Mary was not so naive after all; Godwin's "human reasonableness," which seemed evident in society during the preceding time of prosperity, is revealed to have been only a veneer. Society quickly relapses into mob violence, super-stition, and madness. Religions become even less rational than before. A group of Americans invade Ireland, as if on a Crusade, and a Methodist preacher rants in the streets. Even scientists lose their sanity and die with uncomprehending curses on their lips. Reminiscent of *Frankenstein*, a doomed hero, Verney, begins an obsessive odyssey through several countries; he finds every-where that civilization has disappeared, leaving behind only its sad relics.

Though Mary's endtime does not fall with all the divine fireworks predicted in religious prophecies of the last days, melodramatic natural omens do appear. A black twin of the sun rises one day in the west and meets the true sun in the sky at noon. There are unusual storms; meteors of amazing size, which in ancient literature always portended shattering events, dazzle the night sky.

England quickly loses its characteristic as the natural for-tress so eloquently celebrated by Shakespeare and subsequent po-ets:

> And now the sea, late our defence, seems our prison bound; hemmed in by its gulphs, we shall die like the famished inhabitants of a besieged town. Other nations have a fellowship in death; but we, shut out from all neighbourhood, must bury our own dead, and little Eng-land becomes a wide, wide tomb. (1)

Verney, the last man, laments that mankind is no longer the favorite of his Creator as, for example, that "Royal Psalmist," King David, had once proclaimed. Mary provides Verney, in pas-sages of some eloquence, a sorrowful dirge on the death of Anglo-Saxon civilization. Not only is the "Royal Psalmist" of the Bib-le quoted, but so is Sophocles and even Percy Bysshe Shelley, with a passage from "The Cenci."

Verney visits the abandoned sites of several civilizations, traveling through France and finding it empty of human inhabi-tants. Though he occasionally finds one or two surviving natives in the larger European towns, they roam the streets like ghosts, knowing they are doomed.

Verney has initially embarked with three companions. This British party does reach the "snows of Switzerland" only to find that land too is "desolate of its inhabitants." The frozen mountain fortress is discovered to have been no more a protection against plague than was England's island isolation. The pesti-lence continues its course, lasting a Biblical-style seven years, until it has thoroughly done its work. One of Verney's compan-ions dies of typhus; the other two are lost at sea. Completely alone, Verney continues his journey, hoping to find one living soul for companionship. He visits Venice and a remarkable des-cription of that city, now a splendid mausoleum, is provided.

Verney compares himself, appropriately, to Robinson Crusoe, but finds little comfort there; he has no hope of even a hostile

69

human encounter, finds no Man Friday, and anticipates no rescue. Some living creatures remain—oxen, horses, dogs—but no human beings. Lamenting that he is "sole survivor" of his species, Verney watches night fall and other living creatures seeking the bosom of their mates. He experiences none of the exhilaration of Crusoe's adventure. More alone even than the Frankenstein Monster, Verney envies the animals with their companions and young.

Moving on to Rome, that "majestic and eternal survivor of millions of generations of extinct men," Verney lives for a time in its abandoned, depopulated grandeur. What unfolds is surely one of the most curious fantasies of mastery ever penned. He is lord of the Eternal City. The Vatican Library is his, and magnificent villas of the Roman nobility open their treasures to him. In the granaries of Rome, he finds plenty of food. Yet he finds this living "without love, without sympathy, without community" senseless. Fate has somehow, if with special cruelty, spared him. Refusing to reject this unique gift of life, burden though it be, he seeks an occupation which, he feels, is the only thing that can make his solitude tolerable. Since he is Mary Shelley's character, it is not surprising that he occupies himself by writing his story for a now-empty planet. Mary has, again, rejected suicide as a solution for the misery of her protagonists. Verney will cling to his unique gift of life. With an activity which must ultimately be senseless sustaining him, Verney is indeed the last Sisyphus.

Choosing the Colonna Palace in Rome for his residence, Verney finds only bitterness in the unshared beauty of its paintings and magnificent halls, though he does lose himself in reverie before "fair madonna or beauteous nymph." He rambles the empty streets of the Imperial City. Like the desert island heroes of DeFoe and the heroes of subsequent romances which imitated Crusoe's plight, Verney acquires an animal companion, a shaggy dog he finds tending sheep, as if waiting for its master to return, anxious to be found about its task. As Verney's story ends, he resumes wandering, with the dim hope in his heart that perhaps somewhere hidden on the lonely planet a male and a female may remain to find each other and produce a child who will one day find his manuscript.

The book concludes, in its consistent melancholy voice:

Thus around the shores of deserted earth, while the sun is high and the moon waxes and wanes, angels, the spirits of the dead, and the ever-open eye of the Supreme, will behold the tiny bark, freighted with Verney—the LAST MAN. (2)

The idea of the solitary and supremely self-reliant man—which could sometimes be a family, or a woman, or even a child—was, of course, popular in the literature of Mary's time and retains its appeal even for present-day readers. About twenty years later, in 1845, Henry David Thoreau was to spend his much-documented twenty-six months at Walden Pond in a blessed if somewhat exaggerated isolation. Mary had certainly listened to friends of her father and husband planning their Pantisocracies, where groups of like-minded people would escape the wiles of society to live in creative tranquility. *Robinson Crusoe* (1719) and its many imitations and literary progeny had merely provided an idealized vision of the solitary individual shipwrecked in a natural paradise, taming animals, finding barbarian companions, and surviving.

But Mary saw the solitary survivor with more nightmarish clarity, not being rewarded by benevolent nature but cursed by utter loneliness and the horror of being forced to witness the extinction of his kind. Science-fiction writers have continued to be fascinated by the survivor-hero forced to endure an ugly, devastated earth, from which there is little hope of rescue. Only the more generous writers have provided, then usually tentatively, an Eve through whom the human race at least has a faint chance of survival after cataclysmic devastations.

In his comprehensive and provocative book *New Worlds for Old*, David Ketterer, whose flattering views on the importance of Mary Shelley are well known, examines *The Last Man*. The novel, he suggests, provides transition between the uses of plagues in ancient literature, where they were perceived to be God's punishment for the violation of taboos, and the place of disaster in contemporary fiction, where it is usually the consequence of man's own failure to harness atomic energy, clean up the Earth, restore ecological balance, or make peace among men. Yet in both ancient and modern literature, we might add to Ketterer's observations, the disaster story has generally been a cautionary tale. Man was responsible for alienating the gods, just as he has willingly polluted the Earth. Mary's narrative is different in the absence equally of God's wrath or man's guilt. It is, therefore, in its inexorable movement toward destruction more terrifying than the other tales, both ancient and modern.

W. Warren Wagar, in his *Terminal Visions: The Literature of Last Things*, includes a sustained discussion of *The Last Man*. Acknowledging Brian Aldiss's high commendation of *Frankenstein* as the first authentic work of modern science fiction, a pioneering effort to bring man and his science and technology into significant literary confrontation, Wagar asserts that the "large and somewhat turgid romance" which is *The Last Man* is of equal importance, with "an even stronger claim to consideration [than *Frankenstein*] as the first major example of secular eschatology in literature." (3)

Wagar knows as well as Ketterer that fears for the utter destruction of the human race are indeed ancient, echoed in the Flood narratives of many Near Eastern cultures and in the Biblical stories of Babel and of Sodom and Gomorrah. These calamities were indeed perceived to be the judgment of the gods or of God and therefore preventable by man. Even in medieval times, it was believed that European villages could vow good works in exchange for being spared the ravages of plague. Oberammergau was not only spared but granted perpetual prosperity through its promise to dramatize Christ's Passion. With Mary Shelley, the gods and their quick vengeance have been removed from the heavens, and the primordial fear of impending doom has been secularized. Man feels even more helpless without the gods to at least beseech for mercy. Wager believes that Mary has brilliantly conveyed that sheer terror.

Though Mary learned atheism, anarchism, and the perfectibility of man from her father and her husband, Wagar believes that these ideas did not touch her viscerally, and she never developed a consistent religious philosophy. Her writings and actions, he feels, reveal that she was , innately conservative, despite the early influences of radical family and loved ones. She seems to have cherished the hope of survival after death and comforted herself with references to a personalized deity. Yet, her writings also indicate that she was sufficiently the product of an enlightened domestic and social environment to reject much, if not all, of the religious bigotry and superstition of her period. Wagar believes that when Mary was ready to treat the end of the world in fiction, what emerged philosophically from her was "a mix of influences, abilities and temperaments." Though she occasionally invokes conventional piety and actually appeared to share it from time to time in her personal life, her book is almost totally secular.

Wagar concedes that *The Last Man* is unlikely to ever be regarded as a great work of imaginative literature and will always be overshadowed by *Frankenstein*. But he feels, nevertheless, that "its writing is an event of high significance in the history of secular eschatology and in the history of the secularization of Western consciousness itself." (4) While it is not the first account of a secular doomsday, it is vastly more important than an assortment of less ambitious romantic tales and poems which had a similar subject.

Muriel Spark, the novelist who has often had her quotable say on Mary, stressed the book's social vision. She is not totally incorrect, certainly, in asserting that the book "created an entirely new genre, compounded....of the domestic romance, the Gothic extravaganza, and the sociological novel." (5)

NOTES

1. Hugh J. Luke, Jr., ed., *The Last Man* (Lincoln: University of Nebraska Press, 1965), p. 180.

2. Ibid., p. 342.

3. W. Warren Wagar, *Terminal Visions: The Literature of Last Things* (Bloomington: Indiana University Press, 1982), p. 13.

4. Ibid., p. 16.

5. Muriel Spark, *Child of Light: A Reassessment of Mary Wollstonecraft Shelley* (Hadleigh, UK: Tower Bridge Publications, 1951), p. 2.

VII
GERMINAL FANTASY AND
SCIENCE-FICTION SHORT STORIES

During the early years of her widowhood, spurred on by the necessity of earning a living, Mary produced a number of short stories and sketches. Short fiction could be sold to *The Keepsake*, a commercially successful literary annual that was published in England between 1828 and 1857. *Keepsake* and other similar annuals were sold as gift books and were especially popular as remembrances for birthdays and for the Christmas and New Year holidays. Vividly illustrated with engraved plates, they offered their readers both emotional poetry and dramatic prose fiction. Though professional reviewers sometimes ridiculed the content of the volumes—labeling it sentimental, contrived, trite, and a vulgar pandering to the tastes of the common reader—the annuals did attract some authors of skill. Unfortunately, the lasting influence of the annuals was slight, and they had little if any impact on the development of the short story throughout the nineteenth century.

Mary's writing for *The Keepsake*, though competent, was not highly distinguished. Several of her stories, however, merit attention for her use, thoughtful as always, of ideas that were to become important to fantasy and science-fiction audiences.

"Transformation" reveals something of the way Mary assimilated her literary influences. Its plot was almost certainly derived from Lord Byron's drama *The Deformed Transformed*, which Mary had transcribed for the author. In Byron's drama, a hunchback receives a handsome new body from a diabolical wizard, who then proceeds to follow him, becoming, in fact, his sinister double. Though Byron (whose own club foot presented no problem in charming the ladies) quickly lost interest in his play about a grotesque physical deformity and never bothered to finish it, his hero was, according to his original outline, to have achieved his liberation by slaying the wizard and, in the process, since the wizard had become his shadow, killing himself.

In her version, Mary continued to employ the figure of the *doppelgänger* but substituted a happy ending for the one Byron had intended. Her deformed dwarf takes possession of the body of her hero, Guido, in order to woo Juliet, a young woman Gudio himself has loved since childhood but has lost because of his profligate ways. Guido manages to win his body back from the dwarf and learns a lesson from his adventure that enables him to regain the affections of his loved one. The double is used in an unexpected way. Guido's double, rather than being a fiend who mirrors his darker nature, which was the customary role of the *doppelgänger*, turns out to be a kindly agent in disguise sent to teach Guido a lesson about the harmful effects of pride and vanity. Mary's story, though it has some originality, is less allusive and suspenseful than Edgar Allan Poe's more conventional *doppelgänger* tale, "William Wilson," to which it has been compared. "Transformation," though interesting, does not measure up to the finest stories of its genre.

"The Moral Immortal," which comes as a surprise to those who believe Mary had no sense of humor, may actually be a gentle parody of William Godwin's pompous narrative, *St. Leon*. In Mary's story, the disciple of a master magician surreptitiously drinks an elixir of immortality, mistaking it for a potion guaranteed to cure him of an unhappy love. Though he achieves perpetual youth, he still suffers from lovesickness. Bertha, the woman he loves, ages normally and, after years have passed, becomes a wrinkled old lady, while her suitor, who has finally succeeded in becoming her husband, remains young and handsome. Though the hero has won his beloved, not surprisingly, they both come to abhor their abnormal union. So miserable does life become, that the hero debates the ethics of suicide. Since suicide is never a valid option in Mary's writings, he chooses life and continues his dreary existence until he is mercifully released after three centuries of horrid youth.

While touches of ironic wit and hints of Godwinian parody have led some readers to call "The Moral Immortal" a humorous tale, it is evident that any humor present is dark indeed. There are too many reflections on the tragic transience of life, and there may also be some implied criticism of religious doctrine. Though this could not have been stated openly in *Keepsake*, Mary seems to be saying that eternal life, if we had it, would be a curse. Bertha, beloved of the apprentice, is first a coquette not meant to be admired by the reader. As punishment for her vanity and cruel beauty, she is made to wither with age while her husband, whom she first treated so casually, retains his youthful manliness. The central theme of *Frankenstein* is reiterated in a minor key; the overreacher who tries to acquire the powers that belong to God alone is always punished. Wizards and scientists can quickly go too far. Supernatural events are used in the story not for their titillating effect but to investigate human personality in relation to a theme Mary enjoyed exploring. The thinness of the tale and a troubling inconsistency of tone prevent it from being able to carry the weight of its themes. The Wandering Jew motif is certainly overworked, and the reader feels no profound revelation has been granted in the discovery that, when a silly woman tempts a philosopher's assistant, she does a dangerous thing. Yet because of the popularity of the *elixir vitae* idea in fantasy writing, "The Moral Immortal" has become the most frequently anthologized of all Mary Shelley's stories and one of the few that is still read.

Of special interest to the historian of science fiction are two stories which employ techniques later writers have frequently exploited. "Valerius: The Reanimated Roman," probably written in 1819 (but unpublished until 1976), and "Roger Dodsworth: The Reanimated Englishman," completed in 1816 but not published until 1863, take two characters time-traveling but provide pseudo-scientific explanations for the wonderous events. Despite its use of a central idea of genuine interest to Mary's immediate audience, "Valerius" was not published until Charles Robinson made his collection of the shorter fiction in 1976. It is, therefore, impossible to claim any influence upon the vast number of science-fiction writers who have concocted stories in a similar vein.

"Valerius" has a number of interesting ideas and revealing details. Mary's vision, her much acclaimed "SF imagination," is clearly evident. She has produced a "sleeper" story in which an ancient Roman comes forth into the modern world, not by magic but by a freak of nature, a scientific oddity which Mary characteristically fails to elucidate, though she is at pains to assure her reader that her tale could actually have happened. After being resurrected, Valerius freely gives his opinions on the new world he sees about him and looks with disdain on modern Italians. Not surprisingly, his observations at every point parallel those of his author and other typical English folk of her class who frequented Italy and found the Italians not always behaving according to Anglo-Saxon notions of propriety.

The people Valerius encounters in the sketch, which is more a contemplative narrative or treatise in the form of a thin fiction than a story proper, seem to accept his reanimation as natural and not even particularly unusual. The interest in the story does not reside in the reappearance of Valerius but in his response to his strange "time travel" opportunity to see what has happened to the great empire he left hundreds of years before. The Roman is provided a modern English auditor, to whom he gives little personal information or detailed history of the Roman Republic. Rather, he moralistically, and with a reserve again resembling that of an English person of Mary's own time, explains what it feels like visiting Rome nineteen-hundred years later, seeing the Pantheon again by night, when the rays of the moon fall directly through the opening in the roof of the structure, and the Coliseum, half in ruin, deserted and mournful.

While "Valerius" is a stagnant narrative, it is extremely interesting as an opinionated statement of what Mary believed ancient Roman values to have been as opposed to what she perceived as the decadence of modern Italian life. Valerius first appears with an English gentleman of rank, possibly one of the few people in the modern world to whom this dignified ancient can effectively relate! In appearance, the reader is told, Valerius resembles a statue of Marcus Aurelius. One passage in the narrative seems to suggest that Mary herself must often have gazed at Rome's statues of ancient worthies, wondering what it would be like if they could suddenly return to life and speak to her. Quite clearly, Mary believed they would behave like English gentlemen.

Valerius, Roman Republican that he was, does not hesitate to express his distaste for modern Italians, the descendants of barbarians, in his view, who usurp the noble name of Roman. He laments the decline of patriotism since the days when he heard the voices of Cicero and Cato about the Forum. He talks freely about "this fallen Italy" as he wanders about the ancient ruins. He concludes that all that is great and good has departed. The temples of the gods lie in ruin, as do the decaying columns of the imperial courts. Rome is now filled with "hateful superstition," with the new religion of Christianity, which Valerius finds inferior to Roman paganism in every way. He confides to his English friend (and, rather daringly, to the anticipated *Keepsake* reader as well): "The strangers that possess her [Rome] have lost all the characteristics of Romans; they have fallen off from her holy religion. Modern Rome is the Capital of Christianity, and that title is that which is crown and top of my despair...." (1) He admits to "a great aversion" to the ministers of the new religion and to "Catholic superstition." He is sickened by the "sacrilege" of the conversion of the Pantheon, temple to all the gods, into the church of the One God.

Since the narrative was unpublished until recent times, it is not possible to know how Mary's audience would have reacted to Valerius's attack on Christianity. Perhaps an English audience would have interpreted his remarks as a sound criticism of "Romanist abuses" and taken no offense.

Rather obsessively, Valerius decides to live in the Coliseum and will not leave it. He is deeply unhappy in this strange city where a language is spoken that he can barely understand. Even the discovery of the great Roman writers who lived after his time—Virgil, Horace, Ovid, Lucan, Livy, Tacitus, and Seneca (who would certainly seem worth coming back from the grave to read)—is unable to save him from a living death of despair in the ruins. A Scottish noblewoman develops a filial affection for him (Mary Shelley's father complex surfacing again!) and reflects long on his state of psychological disorientation, which today would be neatly labeled "severe 'future shock'" The narrator, so anti-Italian in sentiment, does also note in passing that if a man from Periclean Athens were to return from the dead to see what remains of classical Greek culture, he would have even greater cause to weep for the fall of his own civilization.

Roger Dodsworth: The Reanimated Englishman

In her second tale of reanimation, which did see publication during her lifetime, Mary admitted through her narrator that she had often entertained herself by conjecturing how particular heroes of antiquity would respond if they were to return in her own time. Having, with some success, reanimated a fictional Roman, she decided to try her hand at resuscitating an Englishman of an earlier era. Certainly her fellow countrymen, who were by no means following the liberating advice of Percy Bysshe Shelley, deserved pronouncement against them by one brought back from their own history.

This second "narrative essay," as it was fittingly called, appears to have been directly inspired by a hoax that originated in France in June of 1826. At least six British newspapers passed on to their readers a report from the *Journal du Commerce de Lyon* of the appearance of a man reanimated from the past. Whether gullibly accepted or not, the idea of such an event appealed to the popular imagination and was even the subject of considerable comment in intellectual circles.

The hoax obviously intrigued Mary, leading her to flirt again imaginatively with the tantalizing possibility of reanimation. Though her narrative was written in 1826, at the time of the hoax, it was not published until 1863. It had been out of print for over a hundred years when Charles Robinson rescued it for his collection of Mary's shorter works. While "Roger Dodsworth" is of interest to science-fiction readers, because of its long unavailability, again as with "Valerius," no direct claim can be made for its relationship to any tales of reanimation by contemporary writers who have produced accounts of time travel or human hibernation.

According to Mary's sketch, Roger Dodsworth was frozen after he was caught in an avalanche. At the time of his inhumation in 1657, he was thirty-seven years old. One-hundred-and-fifty years later, he is found and thawed out. Emerging from his icy grave, he becomes the subject of "romantic wonder and scientific interest." (2) Mary attempts to provide a partial, scientific-sounding account of what happened. The following passage, though excessively verbose, is of special interest to those who wish to understand how her "science-fiction" imagination operated:

Animation (I believe physiologists agree) can as easily be suspended for an hundred and two years, as for as many seconds. A body hermetically sealed up by the frost, is of necessity preserved in its pristine entireness. That which is totally secluded from the action of external agency, can neither have any thing added to nor taken away from it: no decay can take place, or something can never become nothing; under the influence of that state of being which we call death, change but not annihilation removes from our sight the corporeal atoms; the ether receives sustenance from them, the air is fed by them, each element takes its own, thus seizing forcible repayment of what it had lent. But the elements that hovered round Mr. Dodsworth's icy shroud had no power to overcome the obstacle it presented. No zephyr could gather a hair from his head, nor could the influence of dewy night or genial morn penetrate his more than adamantine panoply. The story of the Seven Sleepers rests on a miraculous interposition—they slept. Mr. Dodsworth did not sleep; his breast never heaved, his pulses were stopped; death had his finger pressed on his lips which no breath might pass. He has removed it now, the grim shadow is vanquished, and stands wondering. His victim has cast from him the frosty spell, and arises as perfect a man as he had lain down an hundred and fifty years before. (3)

The quaint preciosity and allusiveness of Mary's style in this passage is as characteristic as her tendency to ask her reader to accept scientific plausibility merely on faith. Dodsworth discovers with some astonishment that the government of England has changed radically during his long sleep. The familiar "objects, thoughts, and habits" of his boyhood are now picturesque antiquities. He is especially grieved to learn that his childhood playmate, who was, as is usually the case in Mary's writings, destined to be his bride, has been dead lo these many years. While nothing really happens in this sketch of a British Rip Van Winkle, there is much proud talk of "this enlightened nineteenth century."

Dodsworth's shock appears hardly as dramatic as was that of Valerius. He finds, in fact, much in modern England he can admire. It is suggested to the reader that, though there may be fewer glorious spirits in the present than in days gone by, Dodsworth will certainly admire English progress in science, marvel at the diffusion of knowledge, and rejoice in the fresh mood of enterprise which characterizes modern people. Dodsworth is likely to preach neither the perfectibility of man nor his total depravity but will remain "the moderate, peaceful, unenthusiastic Mr. Dodsworth that he was in 1647." (4)

Mary Shelley's narrator makes reference, with no extended application or analysis, to a theory outlined by Virgil in the sixth book of the *Aeneid*. Every thousand years, the dead return to life, with the same sensibilities and capacities as before, according to this belief. The reader is reminded that Pythagoras, too, believed he remembered many such transmigrations, although, marvels the narrator, "for a philosopher he made very little use of his anterior memories." (5) Mary's narrator concludes that "if philosophical novels were in fashion, we conceive an excellent one might be written on the development of the same mind in various stations, in different periods of the world's history." (6) Although the narrator does not mention it, it will be recalled that Percy Bysshe also liked to talk about reincarnation. It may also be added that a number of recent writers both in science fiction and in "mainstream" literature have taken up the narrator's suggestion for a philosophical novel.

Mary was wise enough to understand something about the psychological state of disorientation that we today call "future shock." No matter how much finer Mr. Dodsworth might find the brave new world into which he has been projected, he can never be psychologically prepared to deal with it. The sketch ends with a speculation that perhaps the hidden Mr. Dodsworth, whom no one, after all, ever really sees, may indeed already have perished before news of him reached the world. It is suggested that perhaps "his ancient clay could not thrive on the harvests of these latter days." It may even be that Mr. Dodsworth, the reader is told, has returned without any protest to the dark realm from which he had briefly emerged.

NOTES

1. Charles E. Robinson, ed., *Mary Shelley: Collected Tales and Stories* (Baltimore: The Johns Hopkins University Press, 1976), p. 337.

2. Ibid., p. 44.

3. Ibid.

4. Ibid., p. 48.

5. Ibid., p. 49.

6. Ibid.

VIII
OTHER WRITINGS, LARGELY FORGOTTEN

All too often Mary Shelley is regarded as a one-book author. Her importance to the history of science fiction and fantasy is slightly extended when the reader considers *The Last Man* and a few of her short stories, along with *Frankenstein*. It is, however, important for those interested in Mary herself to remember that she was a writer throughout her life, by calling and necessity, and her largely forgotten writings deserve some attention, occasionally for their inherent interest, sometimes for the insights they provide into the live of the Shelleys and their associates, and always for their merit as literary period pieces, which reveal much to students of the era.

Mary's obscure works can be divided roughly into the following groups: minor romances and other fictional works; personal writings; poetry; biography; and, finally, edited materials.

Mathilda

Though it remained in manuscript during Mary's life, because Godwin, for reasons not difficult to determine, refused to make any efforts toward its publication, *Mathilda* is a characteristic work of fiction of its period. Even today, when it is finally achieving publication as a literary curiosity, it is more accessible than many of Mary's other writings and has considerable interest for our own time. Books in the last few years, both fiction and non-fiction, have rediscovered the public's interest in incest, that titillating topic of the Romantic period. Equipped with the Freudian sophistication of our century, we feel ourselves competent to examine literary glimpses of this area of taboo experience. And Mary's *Mathilda* seems almost a case study of the Electra complex, something which she must certainly have known about, steeped as she was in the classics, though innocent through chronology of Freudian terminology.

It is certainly a mistake to read this novelette, as so many are tempted to do, as pure autobiography, even though Mary readily admitted her own "extravagant and romantic attachment" to her father. The heroine of her book certainly adores a father who resembles Godwin in a few ways, and there is another character who provides an even closer resemblance to Shelley. Yet the fictional elements in both portraits greatly outweigh the factual, as a summary of the narrative reveals.

A sexual nausea pervades the novelette, and the temptation is strong here to perceive, only dimly veiled, Mary's disappointment in certain facets of her relationship with Shelley, as well as her feelings of forlorn helplessness over the loss of her infants. *Mathilda*'s interpreters have pointed out, perhaps straining the issue, that both heroine and author have names beginning with the letter "M" and that Mathilda, like Mary herself, spent a part of her childhood in Scotland, in the care of others than her parents.

Yet there may be less significance in these details than might be assumed, for most of the events of the narrative are very unlike Mary's own life. Even his harshest critics would not suggest that Godwin ever behaved like the incestuous father in *Mathilda*. Godwin was a poor man who barely managed to support his family, while Mathilda's father is wealthy, treasuring his fine property and splendid possessions. After losing Mathilda's mother, he broods, travels many years abroad, and finally returns to claim his daughter, who looks remarkably like her deceased mother. (At this point a reader is reminded more of that shocking nursery tale "*Peau d'Aine*" by Charles Perrault than of anything in Godwin's conduct.) At first the relationship between father and daughter is Platonically though passionately loving. Then, the father strangely and cruelly withdraws, as he tries to resist his incestuous feelings. Finally, unable to come to terms with his emotions and filled with the horror of them, he is driven to suicide—that solution of last resort which is so rare in Mary's writing, despite its popularity in the other fiction of the period.

William Godwin, far from being a suicidal type, appears to have been totally free of guilt feelings of any sort. Indeed, after losing Mary's mother, instead of wasting away like a fictional hero, he demonstrated a streak of practicality in domestic relations and promptly set about finding a second wife to rear his daughters.

Mathilda is caught in the classic conflict between a passionate love for her father, which society finds depraved, and a less intense devotion to Woodville, a socially acceptable, calm, and reasonable suitor. When Woodville presents himself to Mathilda, her father seethes in anger. He need, however, have no fear; she is too enamoured of Dad to give any young man much attention.

Woodville, a character widely believed to be based on Shelley's personality, is described as the classically educated son of a poor clergyman. He is identified as one of those persons favored at birth by fortune, endowed with intellect and charm that knows "no bounds" and with "no imperfections, however slight." Mary may indeed have been describing Shelley as he appeared to her adoring eyes when she wrote of Woodville:

> ...he was like a poet of old whom the muses had crowned in his cradle, and on whose lips bees had fed. As he walked among other men he seemed encompassed with a heavenly halo that divided him from and lifted him above them. It was his surpassing beauty, the dazzling

82

fire of his eyes, and his words whose accents wrapt the listener in mute and ecstatic wonder, that made him transcend all others so that before him they appeared only formed to minister to his superior excellence. (1)

Mathilda pines over the suicide note her father leaves, confessing his guilty love for her. When a nameless poet, who glows in the feverish passions of the imagination and rejects any love grounded in reality or reason, comes courting, she is unable to respond with affection, despite her admiration for him. Instead of agreeing to marry him, she proposes another plan of action: why not a suicide pact? The poet politely refuses, explaining, for once sensibly, that if he can bring only a slight moment of happiness to another human being, he has no right to relinquish his life.

Mathilda does die young, in answer to all her prayers. Perishing of a fever brought on by grief, she departs this life fully convinced that she will rejoin her father in a higher realm where their devotion will be blameless. She welcomes death with an erotic joy:

In truth I am in love with death; no maiden ever took more pleasure in the contemplation of her bridal attire than I in fancying my limbs already enwrapt in their shroud: is it not my marriage dress? Alone it will unite me to my father when in an eternal mental union we shall never part. (2)

Instead of looking for autobiographical confession at every turn, it is probably more instructive to examine *Mathilda* as Mary's variation on a popular and shocking topic of the time, both in England and on the Continent. Both "Monk" Lewis, writing Gothic romance in English, and Chateaubriand, writing serious fiction in France, jolted their readers with love declarations between close blood kin, as did scores of lesser writers. Even Shelley had built his historical drama *The Cenci* around the melodramatic events that befell an incestuous Italian Renaissance family.

Mathilda, a fair reader must admit, demonstrates sustained creative energy, less sentimentality than one expects in fiction of this type and period, and a more meaningful working out of a few serious themes than is found in some of Mary's writing that was published during her lifetime. The narrative is cluttered with sentences of a type characteristic of Mary's style at this period of her career: they are long, rambling, and breathless, punctuated by many colons, semi-colons, and dashes. Yet style and content, in this feverish book, have achieved a convincing, if exhausting harmony!

Valperga, Or, The Life and Adventures
of Castruccio, Prince of Lucca

Valperga was Mary's second full-length novel. Although i
is rarely read today, at least one Shelley scholar of the highes
distinction, Frederick L. Jones, has labeled it her stronges
work of fiction. With no modern reprint available, the text i
difficult to find. Therefore, most potential readers will neve
be able to make their own judgments. Contemporary readers, any
how, are likely to find the book too lengthy, with too many o
those elaborate historical digressions which enthusiasts of Si
Walter Scott's novels once did not mind but which we have littl
tolerance for today. The central character of Castruccio wil
also appear unconvincing and unsympathetic.

Mary experienced severe personal problems while writing *Val
perga*, but, since she usually was writing under less than favor
able personal circumstances, she had learned to valiantly com
plete her work on schedule no matter what the current famil
crisis might be. Godwin and Shelley agreed that the new romanc
was stronger writing than *Frankenstein*. It had more literary pre
tentions, and Mary was now writing in an established genre rathe
than inventing a new one. She was following Scott's lead i
producing an elaborately-detailed historical romance. Not onl
did her immediate circle respond favorably to *Valperga*, but mos
of the professional reviewers liked it as well.

Carefully noting the tastes of her time and designing
product for a recognized market, Mary constructed her plot wit
considerable care and set it in medieval Italy. Her own trave
experiences and the poetry of Italian life which she had absorbe
while living there with Shelley served her well. Mary starte
her manuscript in Pisa and further researched the subject durin
her residence in Naples with her husband. Taking, as usua
considerable pride in the accuracy of her historical backgrounds
she carefully listed in her preface the books she had consulted
A leading source was Machiavelli's biography of Castruccio. Shel
ley and Mary, like Machiavelli long before them, had becom
intrigued with the psychology of power, the thirst for it, an
the methods by which it is acquired and maintained. It will b
remembered that a hatred of tyranny was a constant theme i
Shelley's life and poetry. Mary earnestly set about embodyin
this theme, certainly one of the dominant ones of the Romanti
period, in her own narrative.

The finished manuscript was placed in Godwin's hands, a
usual. Mary instructed him to take what he wished from its pro
ceeds. Not only did he help himself to the book's earnings, but
even before releasing the manuscript, he felt entitled to tak
any liberties with it he saw fit. Though it is unlikely that h
tampered extensively, it is now impossible to know how much o
the book is actually Godwin's work. His editing probably im
proved the text, and he may have done no more than limit extra
neous digressions.

Most of the clichés of the historical romance are evident i

Valperga. Emotions are overheated, deeds are violent, and amorous entanglements can be fatal. Castruccio, the Prince of Lucca, was a genuine historical figure; he had been an exile and adventurer, who had liberated his native city and finally become its ruler. In 'Mary's account his betrothed, who bears the off-putting name of Euthanasia, deeply loves him, though her patriotic values soon come into conflict with his, as she witnesses his transformation from a noble hero into a tyrant. Beatrice, an even more vulnerable heroine, also loves Castruccio. Though he seduces and abandons her, she continues to adore him. She finally dies in a delirium, asserting that Evil has inherited the earth. Euthanasia survives but her idealized love for Castruccio is replaced for "grief alone."

To lovers of horror fantasy, the title of the romance will immediately suggest *Walpurgisnacht*. However, Valperga is actually the name of the castle where Euthanasia resides; it symbolizes those pleasures of hearth and domesticity which Castruccio sacrifices to his ruthless ambition.

Mary's understanding of the manners, customs, and opinions of the age still makes quaint and rather amusing reading. She carefully researched the religious travail, heresies, and primitive superstitions of the period. She demonstrates genuine skill in presenting her major themes and weaving their threads. The central conflict is clearly and consistently worked out: Euthanasia struggles between her love of Castruccio and her desire to see liberty prevail in the Italian land. Castruccio, who is first presented as a hero worthy of the love of two women such as Euthanasia and Beatrice, is finally corrupted by his lust for power. His boundless ambition has broken all ties of affection and, at the end, he is a loveless, isolated, and wicked human being.

Because of its central theme and subject matter, *Valperga* has been called Mary's version of *The Cenci*. When the idea for the story came to her, Shelley himself was composing *The Revolt of Islam*, a highly ambitious, major poem in which failure of the French Revolution to realize the idealistic goals of its supporters was a key theme. Political issues were much on the minds of both Shelleys during this period. Godwin had written persuasively of the terrible consequences of "the government of a single person." Shelley had already compared Napoleon, a contemporary figure who horrified and fascinated him, to Castruccio. At this period in their lives Mary, Shelley, and others in their circle found in the violent and dramatic history of Italy the ideal materials with which they could give substance to this theme whioh intrigued them, the corrupting force of power.

The Fortunes of Perkin Warbeck

Mary's second significant historical novel was completed in 1830. Though her theme was essentially the one she explored in *Valperga*, this time she chose British rather than Italian historical materials to show that "conflict between political ambition and the desires of the human heart." While the historical Perkin Warbeck appears to have been a provocatively-complex personality, Mary's characterization of him shows no advance in skill over her portrait of Castruccio. If anything, Perkin is less interesting than her earlier hero, who at least possessed ideological coherence and psychological consistency.

The action begins at the battle of "Bos-Worth Field," that crucial event in British and Tudor history so celebrated by Shakespeare and other creative artists who were ready to bend historical fact without scruple for dramatic purpose. Mary advances the theory, which she apparently accepted and did not merely employ for dramatic effect, that, during the reign of Henry VII, Perkin Warbeck, the boldest pretender to the English throne, is not the imposter history has generally accounted him to have been. He is indeed the legitimate ruler, the son of Edward IV and nephew of Richard III. This youthful prince, so Mary's narrative relates, greatly embellishing known history, is spirited off to the Continent as "Perkin Warbeck." There, while contemplating his lot, the thirst for power grows in him, eventually leading him to sacrifice to his ambition the woman he loves, who happens to be a commoner without station. Sadly rejecting her true and honorable devotion, he advantageously marries Lady Katherine Gordon, mounts an unsuccessful opposition to Henry VI, falls captive, and stands trial in England for treason. There, just as history indeed relates, he is executed in 1499. The novel concludes with a brief account of Lady Katherine's widowed years at Henry VII's court. She is described as leading an active life, while cherishing her husband's memory. The habit of reading Mary's fiction as autobiographical is not easily shaken, and it is not surprising that critics have suggested a parallel between Lady Katherine, who turns out to be a good sort, and the author herself in dignified widowhood.

The events of *Perkin Warbeck* demonstrate a conflict between the spirit of medieval chivalry, with its piety, idealism, and aristocracy, and the more rational and modern revolutionary credo based on social justice and stability. Mary failed meaningfully to exploit the conflicts in Warbeck's personality, as he is torn between the medieval and emerging modern worlds and tormented by contending personal desires. Likewise, his death lacks the poignancy it could have been given by a more accomplished writer. One well imagines how Shakespeare, for example, could have made another "Tudor Passion Play" out of this material, even as he did with *Richard II.*

Perkin Warbeck was obviously influenced by the Waverly novels of Sir Walter Scott and was probably a straightforward attempt to cash in on their popularity. Mary, however, did not succeed in creating the memorable characters and dramatic situations which make Scott a significant figure in English literature long after public tastes have changed. Mary was certainly not fully convincing in her central task of depicting the gradual and plausible transformation of a sensitive youth into a crafty, power-hungry adventurer.

Lodore was issued in 1835, after many frustrating delays by its publisher. The book has received more attention from Shelley scholars than *Perkin Warbeck* for the insufficient reason that it has appeared to offer more biographical gleanings. William A. Walling, one of the soundest of critics, regards *Lodore* as the weakest of all Mary's works of fiction, though he concedes the biographical interest that sends students back to it. Edward Dowden, the famous Shakespearean who was the first important scholar to write a biography of Shelley, alerted these students by his announcement that Mary had used her romance to transmute into fiction a clear period of her life with Shelley. Dowden felt that the book expressed the pain caused by extended separations from Shelley, by his first marriage to Harriet Westbrook, with its bitter consequences, and by his flirtation with Emilia Viviani.

Highly sentimental and devoid of serious ideas, *Lodore* generates its meager interest through the machinery of melodrama. The characters are constantly and needlessly complicating their lives, and it is hard for a reader today to develop much concern for them. Lord Lodore, the central character, is certainly a Byronic hero, whether or not he was intended to represent the poet himself. He weds Cornelia Santerre, widely identified as a fictionalization of Harriet Westbrook. The marriage, however, is wrecked by interfering relatives. Lodore is compelled to leave England because of his disreputable past. He takes Ethel, his infant daughter by Cornelia, with him and settles in the wilderness of America, then a popular place for authors to send their fictional exiles. Twelve years pass and Ethel, presumed to represent Mary herself, grows into a lovely girl, now fifteen. Father and daughter plan to return to Europe where Ethel will surely have a more promising future. Before they are able to depart, however, Lodore is killed while dueling in New York. Two more volumes tiresomely follow, without the presence of the title hero who alone generated some excitement. Ethel marries Edward Villiers, a somewhat too-obvious Shelley figure. Though they have financial difficulties, they persevere through these trials to achieve a comfortable life. To make the work of biographers more tantalizing, the book introduces a second Shelley clone and the daughter of a Neapolitan nobleman, a young woman much resembling Emilia Viviani.

Mary is known to have held lofty views on the writer's task, believing that a novelist should "instruct and elevate" rather than merely amuse. She expressed the fear that too many of her scribbling contemporaries were actually corrupting their readers and not merely failing to edify them. But her own moral intention got mislaid somewhere in *Lodore*, which is too convoluted and awkwardly plotted to sustain interest even as a mere entertainment, much less as an ethical exemplum. Perhaps feeling the need to justify her literary efforts, Mary asserted in a letter to

Charles Ollier that her message in *Lodore* was that all is "vanity...except the genuine affections of the heart." (3)

When the biographical sleuths have exhausted their attempts to unscramble the real personalities from the Shelley circle who were fictionally split and transposed into this meandering narrative, it may be that the most interesting feature of *Lodore* will turn out to be Mary's version of that now-classic literary type so popular during the period and still attractive to modern audiences, "the Byronic hero." After all, few writers of romance knew the prototype, the real Byron, as well as she.

Falkner

Falkner, like *Lodore*, is usually dismissed as another mediocre romance which retains some interest for its thinly-fictionalized autobiographical content. Several serious ideas important to Mary are, nevertheless, embodied in the narrative, and yet another Byronic hero appears.

The plot of *Falkner* is standard for a romance of its period. Elizabeth Raby, the heroine, makes her entrance as a six-year-old orphan with mysterious origins and intimations of high connections. Falkner, the gaunt hero, comes to the quiet village where Elizabeth lives, intending to commit suicide in the grand Werther manner. Elizabeth, by one of those curious coincidences so familiar to readers of Mary's fiction, happens on the spot where he is preparing to end his life and snatches his gun just as he is about to fire. The pair then begin one of Mary's ritualistic rambling pilgrimages, visiting London, Europe, and finally Russia. Falkner is redeemed by Elizabeth's filial love, and no erotic relationship is implied. Elizabeth's origins are, of course, in due time discovered; she is of good family and has the right connections to marry Gerard Neville, who just happens to be the son of a woman Falkner believes he accidentally killed in earlier years. By benevolently overseeing this happy marriage, Falkner is able to come to terms with his guilty past. He settles near the young couple, continuing to love Elizabeth in his paternal fashion.

The plot has many of the standard ingredients of Gothic romance: foundlings of good birth, romances that redress old wrongs, rescues from despair and suicide, and Platonic love relationships. Again, however, Mary has sought to present a serious moral theme. Falkner as a character initially suffers from the sin of excessive pride, and his indifference to others has at least contributed to the death of one human being. In the next stage of his development, he loses all hope: with his despair turned in upon himself, he seeks death. Yet he is rescued not merely by the love of an innocent woman but by his discovery of his own ability to unselfishly love another.

Despite its serious message, Mary appears to have written *Falkner* largely for commercial reasons. *Lodore* had been a success, and there was every reason to expect another romance of the same general type would be equally well received. Market expectations perhaps account for the further exploitation of the Byronic hero, although Mary's disapproval of some of Falkner's actions implies a clear moral criticism of the Byronic and Wertherian protagonists as well as her fascination with them. Her attitude toward Falkner may also reflect the changing tastes of the time: the Victorian era had already begun and Byronic heroes, though still demanded by readers, were on their way out.

No reader aware of Mary's fixation on William Godwin can ignore the heroine's obsessive demand for paternal love. Although young Elizabeth marries happily, the total attention of Falkner seems at least as essential to her as a husband's love. Falkner knows that he must always make his home near hers for either of them to be happy.

Other Short Fiction

Though the short fiction of Mary Shelley, published chiefly in the annuals between 1829 and 1839, usually receives little attention, several of her tales are lively and still readable. They contain interesting bits of social and historical information, charming observations on human nature, tantalizing motifs from Gothic fiction, and occasionally even unexpected touches of humor and satire. From time to time, one of these short narratives will turn up in an anthology of fantasy or science fiction, but they are largely unread today. All the stories that have been clearly attributed to Mary, however, have now been collected and are readily available in the superb edition of Charles Robinson.

Mary is known to have written over two dozen tales and stories. Since she sometimes published anonymously, not all of her short writings have been located and identified, and it should still be possible for enterprising students to locate tales, stories, reviews, and essays whioh have not previously been attributed to her.

For the most part, her tales are highly emotional; they are always genteel. While most are brief, modest sketches, a few are longer and more ambitious, attempting some complexity of character development, an expanded plot, or the presentation of a portentous theme. Some are little more than extended reflections on settings or situations in which there is little action or direct dialogue. Instead, a narrator, either in first or third person, may quickly describe a character or situation, without giving the reader much opportunity for participation in the situation or identification with a character. The use of time is also loose, in no sense adhering to the unities Edgar Allan Poe outlined for the short story. Months or years may be skimmed in a few words. Mary rarely aims for a single impression or calculated impact on the reader.

Slightly less than one-fourth of the stories use Mary's native land as setting. Most are narratives of passionate love and hate set in sixteenth-century France or the Europe of her own time. The short narratives Mary produced are in no major respects atypical of material constantly published in the annuals by a variety of regular contributors. If their author had not otherwise distinguished herself, it is unlikely that Mary's selections would stand out from those of the other writers. If judged by the artistic precepts of short story writing to be developed by Hawthorne, Poe, or Henry James, these tales indeed have very little to commend them.

Some of the pieces were probably written to publication specifications and are perhaps not precisely what Mary would have produced had she been free to write according to her own lights. She is known to have complained to her friends that her publishers' demand for shorter materials made her feel she should learn to convey by intuition rather than written statement. The art of implication, later to be so cleverly developed by twentieth-century novelists trained in journalism, was obviously far from her natural inclinations or skill. Consequently, some of her contributions to the annuals were no more than narrative essays in which she took the opportunity to present personal views, such as her opinion of ancient as opposed to modern Romans. Yet when her publisher allowed it, she was still very willing to produce a long, densely-populated, elaborately-plotted tale with many digressive descriptive passages.

Though a contemporary reader may feel Mary lectures too much in her stories, compared to most contributors to *Keepsake*, she is relatively free of blatant moralizing. Robinson observes that, like Shelley himself, "she disliked overtly didactic literature and preferred to familiarize her readers with 'beautiful idealisms of moral excellence' or, conversely, 'to teach the human heart by showing the effects of moral weakness.'" (2) Considering herself accomplished in the art of enduring deprivations and adversity, Mary acknowledged that she sought in her writings to comfort her readers and help them deal with the sorrows and trials they faced. The short narrative made this goal easier.

Readers perpetually seeking autobiography in Mary Shelley's fiction will not be totally disappointed by the shorter works. Partially in response to the tastes of readers of the annuals, she made a number of her heroines orphans. Her characteristic collection of lonely, misunderstood people is present. "The Parvenue," one of the more interesting stories, is about a marriage that bears some resemblance to the circumstances of her own. In "Recollections of Italy," there is almost certainly a portrait of Shelley. Further characters based on her husband appear in "The Mourner" and "The Bride of Modern Italy." The latter, in fact, closely follows the Emilia Viviani episode in Shelley's amorous life. In writing it, Mary demonstrated that she had reached the point where she could view Shelley's Platonic infatuation for Emilia with more amusement than annoyance.

In his introduction to his 1891 edition of Mary's *Tales and Stories*, Richard Garnett said that "in these little tales [Mary] is her perfect self, and the reader will find not only the entertainment of interesting fiction, but a fair picture of the mind...of a lonely, thwarted, misunderstood woman, who could seldom do herself justice, and whose precise place in the contemporary constellation of genius remains to be determined." (4) Robinson, the latest anthologist, observes that even in 1976 Mary Shelley's position in English literature is still open, but he resists any temptation to read her short fiction, Garnett style, as basic confession.

A summary of the subjects and themes of the short narratives not only reiterates many of Mary's lifelong leading ideas but, since this was popular writing, indicates that she was temperamentally atune to the fictional tastes of the time. In "The Invisible Girl" a young woman is persecuted because of her faithfulness to her true love. "The Parvenue," so often identified as a fictionalization of Mary's own matrimonial situation, is about a poor girl who makes a love match with a wealthy man. The heroine's high-born husband cannot understand the simple habits she chooses to retain, while her own family, intoxicated by what they regard as her brilliant marriage, make unreasonable demands on her husbahd. Every member of the girl's family tries to wring money from her husband who, finally at wit's end, after doing all he feels he can for the family, tells his wife she must choose between him or her relations. Though she loves him dearly, the wife finds she cannot desert her mother. She makes her sad choice. For once a mother rather than a father is the object of unquestioning devotion in Mary's fiction. The husband, after a period of mourning, marries an aristocratic lady and settles into a life of comfort. After the initial wedding and family situation are described, the resemblance of "The Parvenue" to Mary's own life becomes less obvious, but the tale may well be the veiled expression of her outrage, otherwise unspoken, at Godwin's incessant demands upon Shelley.

"The Brother and Sister: An Italian Story" is an overwrought, sentimental tale of Italian intrigue, exile, and family loyalty. "A Tale of the Passions" has a similar Italian setting of exotic intrigue and presents the common English view of noble Italians as a hot-blooded, violent race, out of the pages of Dante. "The Heir of Mondolfa," set in the region of Sorrento, is in plot much like a Chaucerian tale. There is a "patient Griselda" mother and a selfish nobleman father, which, not surprisingly, has been labeled a literary image of Sir Timothy Shelley. "Recollections of Italy" is one of those "narrative essays" in which two English folk discuss Italy, one presenting a realistic picture while the other harbors romantic notions. The behavior of the British living in Italy during the time is vividly and amusingly presented. Furthermore, the sketch provides a compendium of attitudes toward Italy, both pro and con, which can still be found among English-speaking people. "The Sisters of Albano" is about a nun with a melodramatic history and an intimate experience of banditry, while "Ferdinando Eboli: A Tale" is another narrative of passionate political adventure among the Italian nobility. Treachery and intrigue seem to rival love making as the characteristic activity of Mary's Italians, or Italians in general as they appeared in the annuals.

Apart from those suggested by real life episodes and those exploiting Italian lore, the tales and sketches are a mixed bag, not easily categorized. They demonstrate considerable range of interest. "The Mourner" is almost certainly based on melodramatic school tales Shelley told Mary. Classical allusions abound, reflecting Shelley's own conversation. "The False Rhyme," which has interesting satirical elements, tells of high court intrigue, while "The Swiss Peasant" is about the violent repercussions of a *bourgeois* citizen's love for a peasant woman. In "The Dream" a melancholy lady has a love dream, much influenced by contemporary poetry and medieval romance. "The Smuggler and his Family" is a guaranteed tearjerker about an unfortunate marriage, maternal love, and a loyal dog. The story also has Chaucerian echoes and, for a woman of Mary's background, is intriguingly pious. Perhaps it was for her intended audience that she had her characters speak of God and the reunion with loved ones after death. Or, perhaps, she was expressing longings of her own.

Adversity in family life and the tests to which matrimonial love is often put are explored in "The Trial of Love." "The Elder Son" relates how two brothers become rivals for the hand of a wealthy lady. "The Pilgrims" returns to familiar subject matter; a sorrowful widowed nobleman must rear his daughter alone, only to feel himself betrayed when she elopes with his enemy. Mary does, however, manage to contrive a happy ending for this otherwise gloomy story.

"Euphrasia: a Tale of Greece" exploits Greek patriotism, much on the public mind when the tale was published. A military narrative, it develops the well-worn idea that "those whom the gods favor die young." "The Evil Eye" is an especially exotic story about Greeks living in Albania.

"An Eighteenth-Century Tale: A Fragment" is exactly what its title suggests, truly a fragment, though it provides the beginning of what might have become an interesting tale. It demonstrates Mary's occasional tendency to leave promising material before it could really germinate in her mind or be carefully worked out on paper. "The Pole," a final tale of some interest, is generally believed to have been the work of Claire Clairmont, with some modifications by Mary, who saw to its publication. It is known that in later years Mary attempted to find publishers for modest writings by Claire and could sometimes do this only by using her own more prominent name. The tale, blatantly anti-Russian in sentiment, places a distressed young lady, a Polish traveler, and a Russian princess in a basic Italian setting.

Mary's short stories, like her minor novels, provide the record of a literary life pursued seriously and industriously. These writings retain a quaint charm, considerable interest for the literary historian, but little intrinsic merit to catch the attention of the general reader, even when he may chance upon one in an occasional anthology

NOTES

1. Elizabeth Nitchie, ed., *Mathilda* (Chapel Hill: University of North Carolina Press, 1959), pp. 54-55.

2. Ibid., p. 77.

3. Cited by William A. Walling, *Mary Shelley* (Boston: Twayne Publishers, 1972), p. 106.

4. Charles E. Robinson, ed., *Mary Shelley: Collected Tales and Stories* (Baltimore: The Johns Hopkins University Press, 1976), p. xv.

5. Richard Garnett, ed., *Tales and Stories of Mary Wollstonecraft* (London: William Paterson and Co., 1891), p.xi.

IX
LADY OF LETTERS:
BIOGRAPHER AND POET

Lives

Mary Shelley did not think of herself as a "dime novelist, a penny a liner." Though she might write for *Keepsake* to earn a living and might churn out imitations of Sir Walter Scott to maintain herself and her child, her literary aspirations remained serious. One of her goals was to be a biographer of men and women of greatness, to function as a sort of modern Plutarch. Her associates often heard her speak of her intention to write major biographies of her husband and father. Her explanation for her failure ever to realize this ambition made sense; Sir Timothy Shelley was constantly threatening to cut off his meager support for Percy Florence if she attached further notoriety to the family name. Her real motivations for delaying these projects were possibly much different and more complex than she realized, stemming from an ambivalence she could not bring herself to acknowledge. It is, anyhow, unlikely that she would have been successful in viewing either Godwin or Shelley with sufficient detachment to produce a satisfactory biography of one or the other. She would most likely have written worshipful hagiographies that would have confused more than enlightened future biographers of the two men. Yet when it came to lives removed from her own, Mary did, from time to time, practice with some distinction the ancient, revered art of literary biography. Certainly, throughout her career, she sustained an interest in interpreting the lives of high achievers. When she was only seventeen, Mary had started a biography of Jean Baptist Louvet, a French journalist and politician who seemed significant at the time, though today he merits only a footnote or two in French histories of his period. Madame de Stael and the Empress Josephine are known to have interested her in early years as possible subjects, and one wishes she had preserved more exhaustive impressions of these women, if only for the value the sketches would have had as revelations of her own thoughts. Her reminiscences of Lord Byron, which would have been at the least a curiosity and at the most highly valuable, are unfortunately now lost. She did, however, assist others who wrote seriously about the poets of her circle, in this way performing a genuine service to literary history. Yet the work Mary did complete as a biographer deserves some attention, though her more ambitious projects never got off the ground. She wrote five volumes of *Lives* in the Reverend Dionysius Lardner's *Cabinet Cyclopedia*, an extensive and important work of semi-popularization which its publishers referred to as an "analytical catalog." Mary's contributions to this highly ambitious undertaking appeared in the years between 1835 and 1839. It is significant that she was the only woman chosen to participate in Lardner's epic project, a clear sign of her status as a person of letters. The roster of contributors was otherwise a directory of the noted male writers of the time.

Although there were those who ridiculed Lardner's undertaking as an exercise in vulgarization, the *Cyclopedia* was widely regarded as a major publishing event and quickly established itself as a useful biographical reference source. Mary's offerings were consistently competent and occasionally meritorious. As some indication of the scope of her interest and research, she wrote of individuals who lived in four different countries and six different centuries. Her life of Madame de Stael, though not what we would call today a comprehensive study, was fifty pages in length and is perceptive enough to make a present-day reader wish she had done a full-length biography.

Mary chose as subjects for her biographical sketches certain Spanish, Portuguese, and Italian literary and historical figures, such as Petrarch, Boccaccio, Machiavelli, Dante, and Foscolo. Petrarch's consuming love for Laura, which Mary probably interpreted more literally than did the poet, fascinated her, though it is not evident that she understood the religious and courtly love ideals and conventions within which the great Italian poet was operating. She was at a distinct disadvantage when it came to interpreting medieval religiosity, though she empathized fully with the loneliness and Platonic aspiration expressed by the poets of the past.

Mary may not have been the ideal biographer for the more witty and satirical writers, such as Voltaire and Rabelais, though even here it would be easy to underestimate her professional skill. Though her temperament was quite different from theirs and she could not help but find them a trifle coarse, her keen intelligence clearly discerned their sharp, brilliant qualities of mind.

Mary's contributions to the *Cyclopedia* still read well. Her sketches are always informative, and occasionally she writes a phrase that is truly quotable. She holds her own in the select company of *Cyclopedia* authors, men whose names now seem less lustrous beside hers. It is to her credit that she did not often resort to the biographical clichés or easy generalizations that frequently mar writing of this genre. Though there are almost inevitably some passages that read today like obtrusive moralizing, they are fewer than might be expected, considering Mary's period and the fact that from ancient times biography has functioned in part as cautionary tale or moral exemplum.

Several biographical proposals were entertained though never completed. Occasionally they provide surprises, demonstrating irrefutably that Mary was less limited by the circumstances of her time and place than is often assumed. She seems seriously to have contemplated writing a life of the Prophet Mohamet, which would have been strange indeed from her pen, though it certainly would have been interesting. The names of numerous English philosophers and celebrated women of letters and other achievements were suggested to her. Like the biographies of Godwin and Shelley, so long promised, these projects never developed beyond a collection of notes.

The lives she did complete still give witness to both her keen mind and her intense admiration of other achievers. She was never content to merely outline a string of accomplishments or list milestones in the careers of her subjects. She always sought the seemingly insignificant detail which becomes an epiphany of character. Even her novels, it is increasingly recognized, contain effective elements of the biographer's art. Had she written novels in a more realistic age, this skill would have been more evident. Mary was indeed proud of her work in biography. On one occasion, at least, she told a professional associate that she believed she had written better biography than fiction. (1)

Verse

Mary admired Shelley's gift for expressing himself in verse and melody much more than she valued any talents of her own. Lord Byron was another friend and associate whose poetic facility she cherished. It was probably inevitable, considering her *milieu*, that she would herself attempt poetry, though her correspondence indicates that she had a clear assessment of her modest abilities in this form. Nevertheless, she tried her hand at poetic drama, and when Shelley died resorted to verse as the only suitable way of expressing her desolation.

In 1820 Mary attempted two blank-verse dramas, *Proserpine* and *Midas*. They were startlingly faithful adaptations of two famous tales from Ovid's *Metamorphoses*. Considering the seriousness with which Mary approached her writing and the fact that she never fictionalized idly but always strove to express important ideas, her choice of subject matter is worth examining. Certainly there are few more poignant narratives from Greek and Roman mythology than those she chose. Proserpine was the maiden beloved of Pluto, whom he abducted to be his consort in the underworld. She was so mourned by her mother, Cerus, the Earth goddess, that the entire world became barren in anguish until the God of Outer Darkness, arm-twisted by Jupiter, at last agreed for his bride to return to earth for a portion of each year. During this time the Earth would bloom, only to wither again in winter when she returned to the dark realm of her husband. This tale of mother-daughter devotion, which carried deep religious meaning for ancient Eleusinian mystery cults, would have had special psychological appeal for Mary too, who loved classical myths and had never known a mother's love.

King Midas, a greedy tyrant of the sort who intrigued the Shelleys, was another mythical figure with strong appeal as a literary subject. His tragedy was that everything he touched, including his own daughter, turned to gold. One wonders if Mary ever glimpsed Godwin as an anti-Midas. Certainly, the increasingly austere and moralistic Mary saw an opportunity to explore themes important to her and also to provide a frame setting for some lyrics of Percy Bysshe's which she chose to place within her own poetic narrative for publication.

While it is not difficult to understand why Mary chose these two tales from Ovid, her own lack of poetic inspiration considerably reduced their narrative power, archetypal force, and psychological resonance. She made the further serious mistake of inserting Shelley's poems within the context of her own verse, revealing even more searingly the dearth of her powers. *Proserpine*, which closely follows Ovid's marvelous story of the abduction and partial return of the daughter of Ceres, shows Mary as a respectable storyteller but no more than a moderately competent "versifier." *Midas*, which has a father-daughter subplot that should have brought out the best in Mary, is inferior even to *Proserpine*.

As a lyric poet without a sustaining narrative line, Mary was still further enfeebled. The most interesting of her few short poems is "The Choice," her highly-personal lyrical response to Shelley's death. Written in heroic couplets, it is over one-hundred-and-fifty lines in length. A poem of retrospection and self-recrimination, though little originality, it painfully reveals Mary's mingled feelings of loss and guilt at her husband's death. This crude memorial poem seems more sadly personal and confessional than all Mary's letters and journal entries.

It is well known that Mary had endured a period of depression following the loss of her children. During this time, Shelley had complained of her seeming rejection. "The Choice" acknowledges her agonizing feelings of guilt over her treatment of her husband at a time of almost-unendurable personal crisis:

...cold neglect, averted eyes,
That blindly crushed thy soul's fond sacrifice:-
My heart was all thine own,-but yet a shell
Closed in it's core, which seemed Impenetrable,
Till sharp-toothed misery tore the husk in twain,
Which gaping lies, nor may unite again.
Forgive me! let thy love descend in dew
Of soft repentance and regret most true;- (2)

And of her bereaved state she tried to speak with triumphant bravery:

Thou liv'st in Nature, Love, my Memory,
With deathless faith for aye adoring thee,
The wife of Time no more, I wed Eternity. (3)

"A Dirge" was first published in 1831, in *Keepsake*, the annual which initially printed most of Mary's short fiction and was not a stranger to lachrymose verse. The poem was later reprinted in the notes to Mary's edition of her husband's poetry. A reader may, alas, be tempted to suggest that "The Dirge" is an instance of the dire results of verse written during powerful emotion rather than out of the later tranquil reflection on that emotion. Though it reeks with sentimentality and self-pity, Mary regarded "A Dirge" as her best poem. Its subject was again the death of Shelley, and its primary model appears to have been the "Adonais" Shelley himself wrote in response to the death of John Keats. While Shelley's pastoral elegy is one of the most frequently anthologized poems in the language, Mary's is, blessedly, almost forgotten. The following two stanzas convey the quality of the whole:

Ah Woe-ah woe-ah woe
By spirits of the deep
He's cradled on the billow,
To his unwaking sleep.

O list! O list! O list!
The spirits of the deep-
Loud sounds their wail of sorrow
While I for ever weep! (4)

To her credit, Mary acknowledged her limitations as a bard, telling a friend: "I can never write verses except under the influence of a strong sentiment and seldom even then." (5)

NOTES

1. Frederick L. Jones, ed., *Letters of Mary Shelley* (Norman: University of Oklahoma Press, 1946), pp. 92-93.

2. *The Choice, A Poem on Shelley's Death* (Folcraft Library Editions, 1972), lines 32-40.

3. Ibid., lines 119-121.

4. Text found in Jones, pp. 99-100.

5. Ibid., p. 98.

X
CHRONICLER OF THE ROMANTIC MOVEMENT

History of a Six Weeks Tour

Mary's non-fictional, largely-personal writings form a major portion of her legacy, valuable not so much because they come from the author of *Frankenstein* but because she was uniquely situated to observe the inner workings of one of the most important circles of writers in the history of English literature. Even had she never penned fiction, she would have value as a chronicler of the Romantic Movement.

History of a Six Weeks Tour was the first book Mary ever wrote and was composed in collaboration with Percy Bysshe. It is particularly appealing because it details their elopement journey. Published in England in 1817, *History* was actually a refined reworking of parts of the journal the Shelleys made a habit of keeping jointly. It is a prime source for biographers, since the period covered was the most crucial of Mary's life, marking the beginning of her cohabitation with Shelley and the real start of her writing career as well.

History demonstrates real talent at nature writing. The Rhine river, which captivated both Shelleys, particularly at this happy time in their lives, is well described. Since the narrative of their journey, without padding, was really too slim for publication alone, four letters, two by Mary and two by Percy Bysshe, were added; they relate experiences in Europe in 1816. To make the book further respectable as an offering to the public, Shelley's "Mont Blanc" poem was added, though it was philosophically contemplative rather than geographically descriptive and therefore not really in harmony with the tone of the rest of the book. Little more than its title qualified it for inclusion in a travelogue.

That Shelley, already a confident writer, assisted Mary in her first publication is important. He believed in her talent and, as she acknowledged on several occasions, gently nudged her into writing and publishing. Without his encouragement, she at least gives the impression that she might never have presented so much of her writing to the public.

Rambles in Germany and Italy

Travel literature, even when written by otherwise interesting people, can be blandly romantic or meaninglessly impressionistic. It can also be as tedious as the home slides of someone else's vacation. When it is good, however, it can be educational in the most painless way and can provide a genuine expansion of experience. It is best when written by one not only versed in the history and art of the culture visited but able to identify with the traditions of other people and examine foreign scenes with the eye of a poet.

Mary provided considerable background information, historical and political, in her travel writings; often she described places she had researched for her fiction. She believed in being well informed on any subject before she attempted to write about it, and her research was frequently meticulous. Sometimes she was able to provide information not easily obtained elsewhere, since she learned from people in the places she visited, as well as from books. Her writings on Italy, though sometimes wide-eyed and naive, are of particular merit. She had seriously considered the problems of the people of Italy, a land experiencing an identity crisis, and had even set forth, somewhat pretentiously, a program for the country, advocating cultural and political unity as well as independence. Her reactions to the Italians remained strong throughout her life and as ambivalent as those of most English persons, who are fascinated by Latins but also repelled by what is perceived as their emotional extravagance.

Mary gives evidence of the common tendency of the travel writer to romanticize. There is more than a bit of "travel poster prose" in her descriptions. Italian women are breathtakingly beautiful, as she usually describes them, while the Italian men she describes are often scarcely more complex than the "happy peasant" stereotype of Romantic poetry. What Mary disliked in the Italian style—and there was admittedly much that would never please an Englishwoman of her class—was charitably attributed to a misgovernment that did not foster the more noble attributes she was sure were latent in the people.

Some of her descriptive passages are strong, for Mary had a good eye for the scenic, whether manmade or natural. Her art criticism, on the other hand, is embarrassingly amateurish, based on an unsophisticated "adventure of the soul among masterpieces." She was not above the use of the travel cliché when genuine insight did not come, and, despite her efforts, she never demonstrated that ability of the finest travel writers to actually penetrate the culture of which she was writing. Regretably, she was no Jan Morris eloquently conveying the experience of, say, Venice, and her travel writing also lacked any of the intriguing eccentricity of a D.H. Lawrence.

More annoying still is an off-and-on tendency toward "schoolgirl gush." Mary finds some scenes so breathtaking that words fail her; she simply gives up any effort to describe them, which is not very helpful to the reader who is not directly beholding these wonders which leave her speechless. Isolated passages of *Rambles* may still deserve inclusion in anthologies of travel literature, but this is because Mary was an important representative of the Englishwoman of her period and class, in addition to being a celebrity. She does not rank among the truly

100

memorable travel writers whose work expands and enables the reader to glimpse with eyes other than his own.

The Journals

Mary's journal, which has now been expertly edited by Frederick L. Jones, is an indispensable source of information on the Shelleys and their associates. Jones's edition provides an attractive and accessible record of Mary's reading and major activities during the crucial years when she produced her most notable writing. It also provides a partial record of Percy Bysshe's reading as well.

Mary had a habit, not unusual for busy persons, famous or obscure, then or today, of going several days without making any notations at all in her journal. Then, she would frequently make a block entry that summed up the events of the intervening time. For this reason, it is not always possible to determine exact dates for all the activities to which she refers. Another complication of the journal, though an interesting one, is the fact that both Mary and Shelley made entries. Despite these problems, which make the work of editors more lively, the journal material provides a wealth of information about the daily lives of the Shelley household.

Like most authentic journals that were maintained for private use rather than public consumption, Mary's makes for dull sustained reading. It leaves out events of importance, as any human being's personal record is likely to do, while it records seeming irrelevancies. Crucial happenings, such as the sudden death of children, occurred all too frequently in the Shelley home. Yet they may be noted only with such brief but poignant phrases as: "Found my baby dead. Miserable day."

Scandal mongers are invariably disappointed by the journal. It is too laconic, and too much is omitted. The reader is left with many questions. Why is the death of the family favorite, little "Willmouse," not recorded at all? From the pen of a woman whose fiction seems so intensely emotional and often so obviously the expression of personal themes and preoccupations, this journal often has an especially disappointing impersonal tone.

The full extent of Mary's known distaste for her stepsister, Claire Clairmont, is never indicated in the journal, perhaps because Shelley, who had free access to it, savored an association with the two "Godwin girls" and defended both, whatever the extent of his intimacy with Claire may have been. Mary's full response to the sad affair of Harriet Westbrook is also unrecorded, probably for the same reasons, although brief notations do acknowledge Harriet's existence.

Writer's journals sometimes contain plot outlines and ideas for stories germinating in the imagination. A number of reasonably-detailed ghost stories are included in the journal, preserved most probably for likely literary use, and there is ample evidence of the fascination the entire Shelley *menage* had with tales of the occult. Claire Clairmont's adventures with a poltergeist are recorded, though the reader of the journal today would like more information from which to interpret these peculiar visitations, which certainly gained Claire an undue share of Shelley's attention. The journal also indicates when Mary was working on the *Frankenstein* manuscript.

Shelley scholars have long recognized Mary's journal as the single most important source of information about the poet's life, and it has been abundantly used by his major biographers. Only more recently has it become the central document for students of Mary's life as well. It is especially useful in establishing the chronology of events in the daily life of the Shelley household, revealing where they lived, when they arrived at a particular place, and who their associates and visitors were.

Mary was no Lady Mary Wortley Montagu; her journal would never be used in university classes as a model of urbane, refined, and witty style. Mary's journal lacks the freshness of observation and amusing description of incident that makes, for example, the journal of Samuel Pepys a classroom favorite or that of Henry David Thoreau a genuine work of art. It is, of course, unfair to compare an intimate personal record to a contrived exercise in journal form which is intended as a work of art.

Nevertheless, Mary did publish several portions of her journal during her lifetime. *The History of a Six Weeks Tour*, as has been seen, was a revised version of journal entries for a particular period. Other journal extracts were published at different times, in magazines and in essay collections. These were, of course, carefully selected. When she later edited the works of Shelley, there is evidence that Mary relied heavily on her journal to refresh her memory of many events.

Despite its use by Shelley's biographers, the journal contains very little about Shelley's writings. Occasionally there is the simple note: "Shelley writes." But much of what Mary recorded remains of great value. She established the helpful habit of mentioning letters the family received and posted. Perhaps the most treasured journal feature of all was the list she kept of both her own readings and those of her husband. Her own list is believed to be almost complete, though Shelley's is less so, having been erratically recorded. In 1817, for example, Mary included in her list, among other items, two volumes of Lord Chesterfield's letters; Coleridge's Lay Sermon; various memoirs and contemporary novels; Milton's masque, "Comus"; writings by Sir Phillip Sidney; plays by Beaumont and Fletcher; tales of Sir Walter Scott, as well as his novel *Waverly*; Suetonius's life of Julius Caesar; DeFoe's *Journal of the Plague Year*; poetry by Byron; John Davis's *Travels in America*; Godwin's Miscellanies; plays by Ben Jonson; *La Nouvelle Heloise* of Jean-Jacques Rousseau; *Lettres Persienne* by Montesquieu; a novel by Charles Brockden Brown, the American Gothic romancer; and plays by Shakespeare. As if this were not a diverse enough assortment of ancient and modern writings, Mary also read Montaigne's essays, the "Georgics" of Virgil, and even started Dante's *Divine Comedy*, while she was correcting *Frankenstein*. And this was only part of her reading during the period.

Though the tone of the journal is largely matter-of-fact and impersonal, there is sometimes a poignant entry. On November 11, 1822, contemplating her recent loss of Shelley, she writes, "It is better to grieve than not to grieve. Grief at least tells me that I was not always what I am now. I was once selected for happiness; let the memory of that abide by me. You pass by an old ruined house in a desolate lane, and heed it not. But if you hear that that house is haunted by a wild and beautiful spirit, it acquires an interest and a beauty of its own." (1) Contemplating the projected task of her later years, the perpetuation of the memory of Shelley, Mary reflects: "I shall write his life, and thus occupy myself in the only manner from which I can derive consolation. That will be a task that may convey some balm. What though I weep. All is better than inaction and not forgetfulness that never is but an inactivity of remembrance." (2)

In 1882 Mary's son, Sir Percy, with the help of his wife, Lady Jane, privately printed (in a severely limited edition of twelve copies) all the papers from his parents' collection which were felt to have biographical importance. These papers, which appeared in four scarce volumes and were called simply *Shelley and Mary*, have proven priceless to scholars. For this project, Mary's journal entries and the letters both she and Shelley exchanged with their friends and associates were neatly arranged in chronological order. Much of the task of arranging and transcribing had been done by Lady Jane, always a devoted daughter-in-law. In this manner and at this time, the importance of the journal was reaffirmed by those closest to Mary.

The Letters

Mary's letters have recently been edited in two volumes by Betty T. Bennett and are available to anyone interested in the personal or professional correspondence. There are lots of letters, but most are interesting only to the specialist. Mary was no Madame de Sévigné, whose epistles glitter with the excitement of her age. She was not even a particularly amusing or informative correspondent. There is also too much self-pity in these generally melancholy missives for them to carry real charm. They do reveal much about the contacts and activities of Mary and her circle, referred to in all seriousness and honor as "a part of the Elect." Mary's writing is the pervading topic of her letters. She speaks of projects finished, others left unfinished, aspirations, feelings of failure, and dissatisfactions. She mentions frustrating efforts to publish, reactions to reviews, and responses to the opinions of friends. She complains of exhaustion as she strives to meet deadlines. Like most authors, she sometimes misplaces manuscripts, must make tedious revisions, and now and then judges her own efforts too harshly.

The first volume of the letters contains a total of three-hundred and ninety-five, dated from October 25, 1814 to August 31, 1827. Over thirteen-hundred letters are included in the two volumes combined. They reveal at first an uncertain young author who, encouraged by her husband, publishes her first book, *Frankenstein*, anonymously. Later they express the sentiments of a young widow managing as best she can, using her connections with Byron, Charles Lamb, Horace Smith, and even Godwin to get herself before the public. Only gradually, in these letters, is Mary shown gaining enough confidence to negotiate directly with publishers and editors and make her own demands.

The letters reveal, yet another time, Mary's deep, enduring attachment to her father. A few of the earlier letters touch on her rather awkward attempt to please Shelley by carrying on a romance, probably Platonic, with Thomas Jefferson Hogg. This was during the period when Shelley was speaking and writing with heated emotion about the pernicious effects of exclusive matrimonial ties. She speaks of the loss of her children, too, and of her occasional romances after Shelley's death, Platonic, and one senses, not very serious. Reflecting a variety of moods, Mary expresses her excitement over books and the discovery of new ideas. The theatre becomes her favorite entertainment in widowhood. She enjoys opera, art, and the excitements of travel. There is pride in her own work and even more in Shelley's achievement and growing reputation. The letters provide glimpses of her hostility toward her stepsister, Claire, so discreetly hidden even in her journal; her disillusionment over the betrayal of trusted friends; her social and financial pressures; and, as always, her grief.

The period covered by the second volume of letters was a busy one in Mary's professional life. She was no mere languishing widow, despite her expressions of self-pity. Between her thirtieth and forty-third birthdays, she published three novels, revised *Frankenstein*, and wrote numerous short stories, essays, poems, sketches, and short biographies. Self-effacing in tone, she appears genuinely to have believed, as these letters again affirm, that her efforts in preparing new editions of the works of Shelley and Byron were vastly more important than her own writings.

Her friends and correspondents include a number of the best-known figures of her time. The most famous, whose names are still remembered, are Bulwer-Lytton; Disraeli, to whom she writes a slightly patronizing letter filled with maternal advice; Washington Irving, who did not respond to her brief matrimonial interest in him; Prosper Merimée, who apparently proposed to her; General Lafayette; Thomas Moore; and Sir Walter Scott, who remained charitable in his assessment of her literary talents.

The letters show much of the private Mary; she sometimes falls out with friends and is not hesitant to tell them and others when she feels they have disappointed her. As she grew older, she appears to have become more "difficult." Her cosmopolitan background is clearly evident in the few letters written in a serviceable Italian or in imperfect French. Her devotion to the memory of her mother is also apparent. Godwin, demanding and difficult, remains a constant concern and, even after his death, there is the necessity of arranging some pension for his widow. Some views on literature are articulated in the letters. The assertion that she writes verse well only under the influence of strong sentiment and rarely even then is an unusual touch of self-deprecating humor as well as an accurate aesthetic judgment. Mary shows herself a true philosophical Stoic when she confides to a friend that the only pleasure worth having in the world is the society of agreeable, gifted, and congenial friends.

Editions of Shelley's Writings

On numerous occasions, Mary continued to state that her true vocation was to be editor of her husband's writings. Early on, she set to work publishing his poems which had not appeared during his life. Writing tireless notes and prefaces to the various editions of his poetry and prose, she intended to use all her energies to insure that he would achieve his rightful place in English literary history. Her editing work ultimately resulted in four major titles: *Posthumous Poems of Percy Bysshe Shelley*; *The Poetical Works of Percy Bysshe Shelley*, four volumes; *The Poetical Works of Percy Bysshe Shelley*, a one-volume, enlarged edition; and *Essays, Letters from Abroad*, published in two volumes. Muriel Spark has spoken of Mary as an incomparable editor. However, most scholars, beginning with Mary's contemporaries and continuing to the present, have disagreed. There were immediate complaints that she had tampered too much with the texts. It soon became evident that she actually preferred some of Shelley's inferior writings and did not always even recognize his best. She is still held responsible for numerous corruptions that entered the revised text, presumed "improvements" that are only now being finally removed by the best-trained Shelley textual scholars. There was, of course, no sinister intent in Mary's operation; she lacked the training in editorial procedure that is available to scholars of our own time. It is evident that she also lacked the understanding of editorial methods, which was known even to the leading editors of her own period.

Mary had two especially grave faults as an editor: she was careless in establishing a text that was as accurate as it might have been, and she was not above suppressing important information in the interest of family privacy. Sometimes she manipulated a text, thinking she was clarifying an ambiguity or correcting a careless construction made by even so overwhelming a genius as she regarded Shelley to have been. Even less excusable, certainly, were her attempts to popularize some of Shelley's writings by making changes; she always weakened the work in the process. But, in all charity, it should be recalled that the Godwin-Shelley family members always freely revised one another's work and thought little about it. Mary fully believed she was within her rights. Shelley's manuscripts were, furthermore, not always easy to decipher. Even now editors, much better trained if less intimately familiar with the poet's methods, complain of the difficulty of that particular task. William Walling calls attention as an extenuating circumstance to Mary's emotiona state at the time she did most of her editing. Objectivity was never possible for her on the subject of Shelley, even in the best of circumstances.

To Mary's lasting credit, she never lost her confidence that Shelley would be remembered among the masters. And at the time she was doing part of her editorial work, relatively few people believed that he would one day be ranked among the major English poets.

NOTES

1. Frederick J. Jones, ed. *Mary Shelley's Journal* (Norman: University of Oklahoma Press, 1947), p. 185.

2. Ibid.

XI
ENDURING LEGACY

Mary Shelley is lastingly significant as a representative woman of letters of her period, as a member of the English Romantic Movement, and as the author of *Frankenstein*. While *The Last Man* does advance and develop an idea that has since become dear to science-fiction readers, it is certainly *Frankenstein* which has articulated a great modern myth.

Mary may well deserve a higher place than she has thus far achieved in literary histories and not merely as a minor novelist who has greatly influenced popular culture. Sir Walter Scott and Jane Austin, William A. Walling points out in his brief but excellent study of Mary for the Twayne Series, are the novelists who dominate the period in which she lived, and certainly in the sweep of the former and in the intricate psychology, wit, and social perceptiveness of the latter, they far outshine Mary. But what about the other novelists of the period? How many can approximate Mary Shelley's achievement? How many can approach her scope, her grasp of ideas, her variety, originality, and lasting influence? Of course, there is not one.

Walling, however, laments that Mary's development during a life of some duration failed by any reasonable critical standard to fulfill the promise of her youth. *Frankenstein* would be an extraordinary novel from any pen, but particularly from that of an author so young and inexperienced as Mary was when she wrote it. Early in life, from infancy in fact, Mary had been exposed to some of the leading literary minds of her time. As Shelley's wife, she was associated daily with some of England's finest poets, and as his widow and a successful novelist in her own right, salon doors were open to her in England and on the Continent. Any aspiring literary artist would regard the environments in which she lived highly fortunate. Yet the best work she did is her earliest. Her late work is not notable for any development or creative maturity. (1)

It is possible merely to speculate on the reasons why Mary did not live up to her early promise. Because she became "the widow Shelley," it has been assumed that she became too self-effacing to assert herself and too preoccupied with promoting the memory of a dead genius. Always the daughter or wife of persons she revered more highly than she regarded herself, Mary remained somewhat apologetic for her own writings. The mature Mary also lacked the financial resources of a Milton or even a young Percy Bysshe Shelley. Making a living through writing, often by deferring to popular tastes, was more immediately urgent than creating works of art. During her prime years, there was always th∎ sensitivity of Sir Timothy to contend with, and Mary had th∎ further responsibility of rearing and properly educating a so∎ It is also possible that she was, after all, one of those write∎ with only a very limited number of significant ideas, ideas be∎ expressed in the exuberance of youth.

It seems more likely, however, that it was Shelley wh∎ generated the energy that truly inspired her. After he was gon∎ her own well of creativity could not be so easily tapped.

Mary was convinced that her chief claim on the minds an∎ hearts of English-speaking people would always be as the compan∎ ion of the man she felt certain would be justly acclaimed as on∎ of the masters of his country's poetry. Though she was alwa∎ ready to give him credit for his support of her own writin∎ efforts at every point, she may not have fully understood ho∎ necessary his creative mind was to the full unfolding of her own.

It is all too easy, in speculating on what might have bee∎ to underrate Mary's real achievement. She worked with respect∎ able success in a number of forms. Without absurdity, she h∎ been called "Mary, the Mother of Science Fiction." Certainly sh∎ helped establish two sub-genres of science fiction: the apocalyp∎ tic novel and the novel of the mad, obsessed scientist destroye∎ by his creation. Working hard as a writer during most of h∎ adult life, she left behind an ample amount of reasonably goo∎ prose. International in outlook, without too very many hints ∎ English parochialism, she never lost her joy in intellectu∎ discovery.

Yet it is always to *Frankenstein* that we return in discus∎ sing Mary's true contribution. Her creation, the Frankenstei∎ monster, is perhaps one of the five or six best known characte∎ in all fiction. How easy it is to forget that the novel, wit∎ its cranky Gothic machinery, is a book which expresses profound∎ serious themes. Near the end of his life, the fictional Franken∎ stein earnestly admonishes Walton: "Learn from me, if not by m∎ precepts, at least by my example, how dangerous is the acquire∎ ment of knowledge and how much happier that man is who believe∎ his native town to be the world, than he who aspires to becom∎ greater than his nature will allow." (2)

The novel is certainly, on one level, an exemplum illustra∎ ting the ancient lesson that worldly pride goeth before a fal∎ The more personal theme, certainly arising from Mary's own exper∎ ience and addressed to the experience of us all, is expressed b∎ the dejected Monster, who tells his creator: "Everywhere I se∎ bliss from which I alone am irrevocably excluded. I was benevo∎ lent and good; misery made me a fiend. Make me happy, and I sha∎ again be virtuous...." (3)

Having read his Milton, the intellectually gifted Monste∎ sees that even Satan was never alone in his malignant majest∎ Only the Monster made by man is scorned by humans and demon∎ alike. More skilled literary depictions of loneliness certainl∎ abound, but it is hard to think of one that is more devastating∎ total than Mary's.

Frankenstein admittedly, has the many flaws that its critics have so neatly identified, especially when it is viewed by contemporary standards of serious fiction. Some may dismiss it as a poorly constructed narrative of a writer just beginning to learn her craft, as yet unable to successfully handle the themes which she incongruously mingles with outrageously fantastic events. Others may laugh when a grotesque Monster, born only yesterday, quotes Milton, gives lectures on vegetarianism, speaks like a Romantic poet, and mouths Godwinian precepts. Yet the book's mythic power, richness of atmosphere, and thrilling action are rarely forgotten. Most of all, Mary's narrative demands to be taken seriously because its words seem to come from her heart. For all its weaknesses, *Frankenstein* is still the only Gothic novel of its period to survive as a living force in popular art and thought.

Rousseau's concept of the Noble Savage may still stimulate discussion, though the world-weariness of the twentieth century makes us more likely than were many of Mary's circle to believe that there is something innately deviant in the human soul, some chaotic inclination which theologians may call "original sin" and for which psychologists have other names. We have seen enough of traditional societies, and they have been sufficiently documented by anthropologists, to make us sceptical of optimistic descriptions of human savages. We still, however, fiercely debate the wisdom of seeking knowledge that will change our very definition of humanity. Every year science seems to present new possibilities, both exciting and terrifying. The nuclear age, genetic engineering, the cybernetic revolution, the retardation of aging, the transplanting of organs from one species to another, and new methods of human reproduction promise and threaten a future that gives us pause. As developed nations now seek laws to limit the havoc they fear may be done by today's equivalent of "the mad scientist"—as if "the mad politician" were more to be trusted—and their high courts debate the rights of artificially inseminated children and frozen embryos, the image of the Frankenstein monster looms large, and the instinctive feeling of the masses still seems to be: "There are some things it is not meant for man to know or do." Nobody has more vividly embodied this fear in narrative form than Mary Shelley.

NOTES

1. For a succinct and cogent summary of Mary Shelley's career see William A. Walling, *Mary Shelley* (Boston: Twayne Publishers, 1972), pp. 142-143.

2. Harold Bloom, ed., *Frankenstein; or The Modern Prometheus* (New York: The New American Library, 1965), p. 52.

3. Leonard Wolf, ed., *The Annotated Frankenstein* (New York: Clarkson N. Potter, 1977), p. 142.

WORKS BY MARY SHELLEY

NOVELS

Falkner. 3 vols. London: Saunders and Otley, 1837. Adventures of a Byronic hero rescued from a *Werther*-like despair by the affections of a kind child.

The Fortunes of Perkin Warbeck. 3 vols. London: Henry Colburn and Richard Bentley, 1830. A narrative in the manner of Sir Walter Scott based on events in British history.

Frankenstein; or the Modern Prometheus. Ed. Harold Bloom. New York: The New American Library, "Signet Classics," 1965. A fine edition of the 1831 text with interesting introductory discussion of relevance of Promethean myth to the Shelley narrative.

The Annotated Frankenstein. Ed. Leonard Wolf. Art by Marcia Huyette. New York: Clarkson N. Potter, Inc., 1977. A big, attractive collection of Frankenstein lore and a readable text of the 1818 edition. Introduction and textual notes extremely helpful. Edition is source of majority of quotes used in present discussion.

Mary Wollstonecraft Shelley's Frankenstein. Illustrated By Berni Wrightson. Introduced by Stephen King. New York: Dodd, Mead, 1983. An elegantly illustrated coffee table edition of the novel, with helpful introductory remarks by King.

The Last Man. Ed. Lugh J. Luke, Jr. Lincoln: University of Nebraska Press, 1965. Novel about destruction by plague of all but one member of human race.

Lodore. New York: Wallis and Newell, 1835. Adventures of another Byronic hero and additional characters presumed to represent members of the Shelley circle.

Valperga: or, the Life and Adventures of Castruccio, Prince of Lucca. 3 vols. London: G. and W.B. Whittaker, 1823. Narrative based on episodes from Italian history, in style of Sir Walter Scott.

SHORTER FICTION

Mary Shelley: Collected Tales and Stories. Ed. Charles E. Robinson. Baltimore: The Johns Hopkins University Press, 1976. A superbly edited collection of Mary's short narratives, most published originally in *The Keepsake.* Excellent notes and a balanced overview of the author's career provided in introduction.

Mathilda. Ed. Elizabeth Nitchie. Chapel Hill: University of North Carolina Press, 1959. Useful edition of curious early short novel which did not see publication during Mary's life, probably because of incestuous love interest.

VERSE

Proserpine and Midas: Two Unpublished Mythological Dramas. Ed. A. Koszul. London: Humphrey Milford, 1922. Significant if undistinguished dramatic poems, demonstrating interest Mary Shelley shared with entire Shelley circle. Material based on Ovid.

The Choice. A Poem on Shelley's Death. Folcraft Library Editions, Limited to 150 oopies, 1972. Autobiographical poem Mary wrote to ease her pain at Shelley's death.

NONFICTION

History of a Six Weeks' Tour through a Part of France. Switzerland, Germany, and Holland: with Letters Descriptive of a Sail Round the Lake of Geneva, and the Glaciers of Chamouni. London: T. Hookham and C. and J. Ollier, 1817. Typical travel writing of Mary Shelley. Adequate descriptions of places visited. Conventional travel literature of the period.

Mary Shelley's Journal. Ed. Frederick J. Jones. Norman: University of Oklahoma Press, 1947. A fine edition of the chief source of information about the daily activities of the Shelleys. Lists of their reading.

The Letters of Mary Wollstonecraft Shelley. Ed. Betty T. Bennett. 2 vols. Baltimore: The Johns Hopkins University Press, 1980. Letters, neither intimate nor literary, revealing Mary's place in literary circles of the time and her friendship with important literary and political figures.

The Letters of Mary W. Shelley. Ed. Frederick L. Jones. 2 vols. Norman: University of Oklahoma Press, 1946. Earlier collection of Mary's letters, with informative editing.

Lives of the Most Eminent Literary and Scientific Men of France. 2 vols. London: Longman, Orme, Brown, Green, Longmans, and John Taylor, 1838-39. A part of Mary's contribution to Lardner's *Cabinet Cyclopaedia*, which itself appeared in a total of 133 volumes.

Lives of the Most Important Literary and Scientific Men of Italy, Spain, and Portugal. 3 vols. London: Longman, Brown, Green, and

Longmans, 1835-37. The rest of Mary's contribution to Lardner's *Cabinet Cyclopaedia.*

Preface. *Essays, Letters from Abroad, Translations and Fragments by Percy Bysshe Shelley.* 2 vols. London: Edward Moxon, 1840. Mary's prefaces to edited works of her husband.

Prefaces and Notes. *The Complete Poetical Works of Percy Bysshe Shelley.* Ed. Thomas Hutchison. London: Oxford Press reprint, 1965. Prefaces and annotations that Mary wrote for Shelley's poetry.

Rambles in Germany and Italy in 1840, 1842, and 1843. 2 vols. London: Edward Moxon, 1844. Additional travel writings, of uneven quality.

BOOKS FOR ADDITIONAL READING

Aldiss, Brian W. *Billion Year Spree: The True History of Science Fiction.* New York: Schocken Books, 1974. One of the most readable histories of science fiction, by distinguished British writer of SF. Gives Mary credit for founding the genre and devotes first chapter to her.

Aldiss, Brian W. *Frankenstein Unbound.* New York: Random House, 1973. Interesting work of fiction generated by *Frankenstein,* in which historical and fictional personalities intermingle.

Bailey, J.O. *Pilgrims Through Space and Time.* Westport, CT: Greenwood Press, 1972. Account of union of Gothic sensibility and scientific world view to produce *Frankenstein.* Discussion of influences on *The Last Man.* An early, classic history of science fiction.

Baxter, John. *Hollywood in the Thirties.* New York: Coronet Paperback Library, 1970. Lively, if thin, survey of movies of the decade. Designates *Frankenstein* of James Whale the most famous horror film and its director the grand master of the film genre. Appropriately illustrated with film stills.

Baxter, John. *Science Fiction in the Cinema.* New York: Warner Paperback Library, 1974. A sound overview of science fiction films, placing Universal Studios' *Frankenstein* within the traditions of Germanic horror rather than SF. Clarifies for discussion basic issues of the two film genres.

Bigland, Eileen. *Mary Shelley.* New York: Appleton-Century-Crofts, Inc., 1959. Adequate survey of background, relationships, and writings of Mary, avoiding pedantry or speculation. Not deeply insightful, but interesting. Biographical rather than critical.

Brown, Ford K. *The Life of William Godwin.* London: J.M. Dent and Sons, 1926. Though not the newest, still probably the best biography of Mary's father. A fair, balanced treatment.

Butler, Ivan. *Horror in the Cinema.* New York: Warner Paperback Library, 1972. A readable, informed survey of horror films with perceptive statements about all the major films inspired by *Frankenstein.*

Carter, Paul A. *The Creation of Tomorrow: Fifty Years of Magazine Fiction.* New York: Columbia University Press, 1977. Good discussion of Frankenstein's monster, humanoids, and robots and the way Mary Shelley's novel influenced magazine science fiction.

Clarens, Carlos. *An Illustrated History of the Horror Film.* New York: A Paragon Book, 1967. A brief but perceptive survey of the Frankenstein films. Good comparisons with other horror films. Not as well illustrated as title would suggest.

Douglas, Drake. *Horror!* New York: Collier Books, 1969. More chatty than scholarly, yet of some value as a popular survey of horror films. Good analysis of character of Victor Frankenstein in the Universal films. Written as a dramatized narrative.

Dowden, Edward. *The Life of Percy Bysshe Shelley.* 2 vols. London: Kegan Paul, Trench and Co., 1886. Once the standard biography of Shelley and still highly readable and useful, though superseded.

Dunn, Jane. *Moon in Eclipse: A Life of Mary Shelley.* New York: St. Martin's Press, 1978. Provocative ideas and a lively style.

Edwards, Anne. *Haunted Summer.* New York: Coward, McCann and Geoghegan, 1972. A novel inspired by the Shelley-Byron circle and the Geneva summer which produced *Frankenstein.* One of the more interesting novels based on the Shelleys and their friends.

Florescu, Radu. *In Search of Frankenstein.* With Contributions by Alan Barbour and Matei Cazacu. Boston: New York Graphic Society, 1975. Also New York: Warner Books, Inc., 1976. A popular, entertaining examination of all manner of Frankenstein lore. Questionable attempts to find connections with Dracula tales and occasionally a strained thesis. Yet good work of popular exploration. Fun to read. Fine filmography.

Glut, Donald F. *Listing of Novels, Translations, Adaptations, Stories, Critical Works, Popular Articles, Series, Fumetti, Verse, Stage Plays, Films, Cartoons, Puppetry, Radio and Television Programs, Comics, Satire and Humor, Spoken and Musical Recordings, Tapes, and Sheet Music Featuring Frankenstein's Monster And/Or Descending from Mary Shelley's Novel* Jefferson, NC:

113

McFarland, 1984. An amusing, compulsive, yet informative collection of Frankenstein trivia. Five hundred and twenty-five pages of illustrated Monster lore. Fun!

Grylls, R. Glynn. *Mary Shelley: A Biography.* New York: Haskell House Publishers, 1969. A thorough, balanced, and interesting biography, concentrating on the years before Shelley's death. Well-documented and researched. Possibly the best biography available.

Harris, Janet. *The Woman Who Created Frankenstein: A Portrait of Mary Shelley.* New York: Harper and Row Publishers, 1979. A gushing, superficial, cliché-ridden biography, mentioned only because it is readily available and better than nothing.

Holmes, Richard. *Shelley: The Pursuit.* New York: E.P. Dutton and Co., 1975. A comprehensive, highly-readable biography of Percy Bysshe Shelley, which gives adequate attention to the role of Mary in his life. Highly critical of Shelley as a person, stressing his self-absorption at the expense of others.

Isherwood, Christopher, and Don Bachardy. *Frankenstein: The True Story.* New York: Avon, 1973. One of the most interesting free "adaptations." An original teleplay exploring several serious ideas left untouched in Mary's classic novel, to which it pays homage. Not "the true story" if faithfulness to the original text is implied.

Ketterer, David. *Frankenstein's Creation: The Book, The Monster, and Human Reality.* Victoria: University of Victoria, 1979. A learned but jargon-laden book, containing useful background information. Excellent overview of influences operating upon Mary when she created the novel.

Ketterer, David. *New Worlds for Old.* Garden City: A Doubleday Anchor Original, 1974. Interesting comments on place of *The Last Man* in the literature of the apocalyptic imagination. A wide-sweeping survey of American literature, with a strained though provocative thesis and the well-supported view that "science fiction is as endemically American as the western."

King, Stephen. *Danse Macabre.* New York: Berkley Books, 1983. Rambling, impressionistic survey of horror writing, by the popular American novelist. Regards *Frankenstein* as germinal writing which has become part of the "American myth pool." Witty comments on the novel and the films it inspired.

Leighton, Margaret. *Shelley's Mary: A Life of Mary Godwin Shelley.* New York: Farrar, Straus and Giroux, 1973. A sensibly interpretive biography, despite its cloying title, designed primarily for young readers of approximately junior high age but of value to a broader audience. Avoids overembellishment or invention of fictional incidents or conversations. Lacks heavy documentation.

Levine, George, and U.C. Knoepflmacher. *The Endurance of Frankenstein: Essays on Mary Shelley's Novel.* Berkeley: University of California Press, 1979. An indispensable collection of essays on the novel, including:

"The Ambiguous Heritage of *Frankenstein*, by George Levine
"*Frankenstein* as Mystery Play," by Judith Wilt
"Fire and Ice in *Frankenstein*," by Andrew Griffin
"Female Gothic," by Ellen Moers
"Thoughts on the Aggression of Daughters," U.C. Knoepflmacher
"Monsters in the Garden: Mary Shelley and the Bourgeois Family," by Kate Ellis
"Mary Shelley's Monster: Politics and Psyche in *Frankenstein*," by Lee Sterrenburg
"Vital Artifice: Mary, Percy and the Psychopolitical Integrity of *Frankenstein*," by Peter Dale Scott
"'Godlike Science/Unhallowed Arts': Language, Nature, and Monstrosity," by Peter Brooks
"*Frankenstein* and Comedy," by Philip Stevick
"The Stage and Film Children of *Frankenstein*: A Survey," by Albert J. Lavalley
"Coming to Life: *Frankenstein* and the Nature of Film Narrative," by William Nestrick

Lyles, W. H. *Mary Shelley: An Annotated Bibliography.* New York: Garland Publishing, Inc., 1975. The prime reference source for the serious student. Comprehensive, critical, and informative. Includes reviews of works that mention Mary even only briefly. Annotations especially helpful.

Moore, Darrell. *The Best, Worst, and Most Unusual: Horror Films.* New York: Beekman House, 1983. Eccentric but entertaining critiques of all major horror films. Lavishly and gruesomely illustrated. Sees the first Universal Studios' *Frankenstein* as a cultural phenomenon, the work of a great director and a great actor, "the most famous horror film of all time."

Neumann, Bonnie Rayford. *The Lonely Muse: A Critical Biography of Mary Wollstonecraft Shelley.* Salzburg, Austria: Institut für Angelstik und Amerikanistik, 1979. A sound reassessment of the use of themes and techniques associated with the Romantic Movement.

Nitchie, Elizabeth. *Mary Shelley: Author of Frankenstein.* New Brunswick: Rutgers University Press, 1953. One of the finest critical studies of the woman and her writings. Perceptive discussion of popularity of novel and its theatrical adaptations.

Norman, Sylva. *Flight of the Skylark; The Development of Shel-*

ley's Reputation. Norman: University of Oklahoma Press, 1954. Examination of responses to Shelley's writings after his death, with attention to Mary's role in promoting his reputation and her fortunes—and misfortunes—in widowhood. Discusses matters which generate much literary gossip, including Mary's "crush" on Washington Irving. Looks at the Shelley societies. Perhaps the best source of information on Mary's widowhood, though treatment of the entire "Elite Circle" is cynical.

Palacio, Jean de. *Mary Shelley dans son oeuvre: contributions aux études shelleyannes.* Paris: Éditions Klincksieck, 1969. Full critical examinations of Mary's writings from historical, biographical, psychological, and textual approaches. Excellent bibliography. Most comprehensive study in any language. Highly recommended to those who can read French.

Parrinder, Patrick. *Science Fiction: Its Criticism and Teaching.* New York: Methuen, 1980. Perceptive description of stylistic features of *Frankenstein* and their relationship to subsequent science fiction writings.

Philmus, Robert M. *Into the Unknown.* Berkeley: University of California Press, 1983. Stresses Mary Shelley's ignorance of science. Explores Godwinian psychological and ethical ideas reflected in *Frankenstein.*

Pitts, Michael. *Horror Film Stars.* Jefferson, North Carolina: McFarland and Company, 1981. Helpful sketch of career of Boris Karloff, with special attention, naturally, to Frankenstein films. A readable book for film enthusiasts.

Poston, Carol H., ed. *A Vindication of the Rights of Woman by Mary Wollstonecraft.* New York: W.W. Norton and Company, 1975. A fine Norton Critical Edition, containing text, background essays, a selection of criticism, a Wollstonecraft chronology, and a selected bibliography of materials pertaining to the mother of Mary Shelley.

Prawer, S.S. *Caligari's Children: The Film as Tale of Terror.* New York: Oxford University Press, 1980. Well-written, highly-acclaimed survey of horror films. Penetrating comments, especially on the Frankenstein films, which it places within earlier dramatic traditions of stage and cinema. Brief but good comparisons of Cooke and Karloff in role of Monster. One of the most scholarly surveys of a cinema genre.

Scholes, Robert, and Eric S. Rabkin. *Science Fiction: History, Science, Vision.* New York: Oxford University Press, 1977. Exploration of philosophical and mythical dimensions of *Frankenstein.* Asserts that Mary created science fiction out of the Gothic thriller by making the fantastic plausible with reference to scientific speculation of her time. Fresh, informed way of presenting familiar idea.

Searles, Baird, Martin Last, Beth Meacham & Michael Franklin. *A Reader's Guide to Science Fiction*. New York: Avon, 1979. Addresses author of *Frankenstei* as "Hail Mary, Mother of science fiction." Includes a chapter entitled "The Spawn of Frankenstein."

El-Shater, Safan. *The Novels of Mary Shelley*. Salzburg, Austria: Institut für Anglestik und Amerikanistik, 1977. Sees *Frankenstein* as a personal expression of the pride, guilt, and loneliness of Mary Shelley's life. Intelligent, if not fully convincing in assessment of the novels.

Shelley, Percy Bysshe. *Shelley's Prose: or, The Trumpet of a Prophecy*. Ed. David Lee Clark. 2nd ed. Albuquerque: University of New Mexico Press, 1966. An almost complete selection of Shelley's prose, well annotated. Sources of several of the ideas Mary developed in her writings revealed here.

Small, Christopher. *Mary Shelley's Frankenstein; Tracing the Myth*. Pittsburgh: University of Pittsburgh Press, 1972. Though tediously written, a thorough inquiry into what the author calls "origins, changes, tendencies, and implications of certain persistent elements in both the 'popular' and 'literary' imagination which appears to concentrate themselves in the work in view."

Solomon, Barbara H., and Paula S. Berggren. *A Mary Wollstonecraft Reader*. New York: New American Library, 1983. An excellent introduction to Wollstonecraft and a judicious selection from her works. Fine critical prefaces to each selection and an interesting, informative introduction.

Spark, Muriel. *Child of Light; A Reassessment of Mary Wollstonecraft Shelley*. Hadleigh: Tower Bridge Publications, 1951. Lively recapitulation of biographical facts and interesting, sometimes curious interpretations of writings, provided by a famous novelist. Stylistically pleasing. Contains abridged version of *The Last Man*. Especially interesting in comparison of Mary's writings to those of Poe.

Tomalin, Claire. *The Life and Death of Mary Wollstonecraft*. New York: New American Library, 1974. A readable, informative biography of the mother of Mary Shelley and an analysis of her contributions to literature and thought. Full drama and irony of an unusual woman's life revealed.

Tropp, Martin. *Mary Shelley's Monster; The Story of "Frankenstein"*. Boston: Houghton Mifflin Co., 1976. Lively style and provocative ideas. Good background on origins of tale. Information about stage and theatre versions of tale.

Wagar, W. Warren. *Terminal Visions: The Literature of Last*

Things. Bloomington: Indiana University Press, 1982. A balanced look at apocalyptic literature with theological insights provided. Fine critical discussion of central ideas of *The Last Man*.

Walling, William A. *Mary Shelley*. Boston: Twayne Publishers, 1972. The single best brief biography and critical study in English. Sound, concise, thorough within its limits, and well-written. Provides a fair assessment of subject. Excellent notes.

White, Newman Ivey. *Shelley*. 2 vols. New York: Alfred A. Knopf, 1940. A thorough, reliable treatment. One of the finest biographies of a Romantic poet.

ARTICLES

Forry, Steven Earl. "*Frankenstein* and the Hideous Progenies of Richard Brinsley Peake," Unpublished paper delivered at International Conference on the Fantastic in Literature, Boca Raton, Florida, 1984. A witty review of the two sources, 19th-century Gothic romance and twentieth-century cinematic melodrama, which created Universal Studios' *Frankenstein*. Meaningful observations of traditions employed or established by the stage productions of *Frankenstein*.

Kmetz, Gail. "Last Women: Mary Shelley in the Shadow of *Frankenstein*," *Ms.*, 3 (February 1975), 12-16. A readable introduction to the subject, from a feminist point-of-view, with no original insights.

Peck, Walter Edwin. "The Biographical Element in the Novels of Mary Wollstonecraft Shelley," *Publication of the Modern Language Association*, 37 (1923), 196-219. Provocative investigation of Mary's novels for portraits of Shelley, Byron, Godwin, Claire Clairmont, and other members of the "elect circle."

Spark, Muriel. "Mary Shelley; A Prophetic Novelist," *The Listener*, 45 (February 22, 1951), 305-6. Stimulating observations of lasting importance of *Frankenstein* and *The Last Man* by a witty admirer of Mary Shelley.

Vlasopolos, Anca. "*Frankenstein*'s Hidden Skeleton: The Psycho-Politics of Oppression," *Science-Fiction Studies*, 10. Part 2 (July 1983), 125. *Frankenstein* viewed as novel of dispossessed of Earth, protesting benefits of rank and class. Hidden logic of book believed to rest on "fusion of the socio-political with the private drama of a man who sees himself as ineluctably driven to incest." Forced Socialist interpretation, but perceptive observations.

INDEX

121